"The greatest danger for most of us is not that our aim is too high and we miss it, but that our aim is too low and we reach it."
MICHAELANGELO

"You can't go back and change the beginning, but you can start where you are and change the ending."
C.S. LEWIS

> **For Lilli, who knows more about human behavior than anyone I know.**

Autism's Declaration of Independence
Navigating Autism in the Age of Uncertainty
Written by Gary S. Mayerson

Copyright ©2020 Gary S. Mayerson

Published by:
Different Roads to Learning, Inc.
121 West 27th Street, Suite 1003B New York, NY 10001
tel: 212.604.9637 | fax: 212.206.9329
www.difflearn.com

All rights reserved. Permission is granted for the user to photocopy limited excerpts for instructional use only (not for resale or other commercial use). No other part of the material protected by this copyright notice may be reproduced or used in any form or by any means, electronic or mechanical, including photocopying and recording or by any information storage and retrieval system without prior written permission by the copyright owners.

Cover and Design by Melissa DiPeri Designs

Printed in the United States
ISBN Number: 978-0-9910403-4-6
Library of Congress Number: 2020933387

AUTISM'S DECLARATION OF INDEPENDENCE
NAVIGATING AUTISM IN THE AGE OF UNCERTAINTY

© **GARY S. MAYERSON 2020**

Table of Contents

Introduction—Welcome To The Age Of Uncertainty 1
About the Author 5
Acknowledgements 7
A Note on Client Confidentiality 9

PART I – Knowing Your Child's Rights and How to Apply Them 11

Chapter 1
The Autism Diagnosis and Its Impact on the Family 13
Are We Really Seeing an Autism "Tsunami?" 14
Obstacle Courses Parents Will Need to Navigate 15
The Special Language Used in the Land of Special Education 15
Preventing or Neutralizing Disagreement with Quality Evaluations 16
Conflict with the School District is Often Avoidable 16
Why Promoting Greater Independence Before Adulthood is Critical 17
The Autism "Refugee Crisis" 18
Autism "Acceptance" Goes Only So Far 19
How to Weigh the Non-Financial Costs 20
Keeping Classic Academics in Its Proper Perspective 21
Two Early Lawsuits Regarding the Efficacy of ABA Interventions 22
Making Plan B Work 29

Chapter 2
What Does the Right to a "Free and Appropriate" Public Education Mean for My Child? 33
The Impact of The Supreme Court's 2017 Groundbreaking Decision in *Endrew F.* 34

Chapter 3
Generalization: The Critical "Missing Link" to Promote Independence and Self-Sufficiency 37

Chapter 4
Managing Your Child's Right to Be Educated in the "Least Restrictive Environment" 43
One Mother's Story 43
What is the "Least Restrictive Environment? 45

Chapter 5
How Parents Can Obtain Independent Evaluations at School District Expense 51

Chapter 6
How Parents Can Manage and Shape the IEP Process 57
Be Aware of Sequence Changes and Evidence of Predetermination 57
Preserve Any Evidence of Intimidation Tactics 59
Should Parents Ever Record Their IEP Meetings? 60
Some Sources of Conflict at IEP Meetings 60
Should Parents Ever Send Their Child to School with a Concealed Recording Device? 62
Parents Should Normally Consent to School District Assessment Requests 62
Choosing the Appropriate IEP Classification 63
Developing Behavior Plans 64
Developing Ambitious and Challenging IEP Goals 64
Developing IEP Goals That Address ADL Skills 64
Developing IEP Goals To Address And Build COVID-19 Safety Skills 64
Managing and Fading Prompting Levels 65
Making a Case for Reasonable Accommodations and Other Classroom Supports 65
Maximizing Access to the Regular Curriculum 66
The Importance of Putting Extracurricular Activities on the IEP 67
The School District's Obligation to Consider Parental Requests In Good Faith 68
How Parents Should Address Concerns About Bullying at the IEP Level 68
Communicating and Documenting Disagreement—Without Being Disagreeable 72
Always Focus on Your Child's Needs 72
What are the Differences Between an IEP and a Section 504 Plan? 73

Chapter 7
Considering Claims Against School Districts—What Relief is Available? 77
Can The COVID-19 Pandemic Give Rise To Any Claims? 78
The Requirement to Send a "10-Day Letter" 78

Chapter 8
When All Else Fails—Filing For an Impartial Hearing (Due Process) 83
Litigating a Case Against the District's "Teacher of the Year" 84
Do Parents Always Need to Hire Counsel to File for Due Process? 85
Preserving and Invoking Your Child's "Pendency" Entitlements 85
Settlement Considerations 86
Why Multi-Year Settlements Should Always Be Reviewed by Counsel 87

The "Unsigning Bonus" 88
The Right to Recover Attorneys' Fees as a "Prevailing Party" 88
When the School District Makes an "Offer of Judgment" 89
How Should Parents Account for Insurance Benefits 90
Gift or Loan—Which Makes the Most Sense? 91
Are Parents Ever Required to Pay the School District's Attorneys' Fees? 91

Chapter 9
Managing Safety Considerations 95
The "Elopement" Threat 95
Fire and Lockdown Drills 96
The COVID-19 Related Threat Of An Infectious School Environment 98
When Your Child Is Coming Home (Or Going to School) with Unexplained Injuries 98
The Potential Danger of Police Encounters 99
Managing the Threat of Food Allergies 108
How to Manage Seizure Activity—The Seizure Action Plan 108
Managing Medications 109
How Parents Should Respond to Evidence of Bullying 109
How Parents Should Respond to Evidence of Sexual Abuse 112

Chapter 10
Dealing with Suspensions and Other Disciplinary Proceedings 121
The Zero-Tolerance Policy that Went Too Far 122
Inappropriate Physical Contact 123
Plagiarism and Other Acts of Academic Dishonesty 123

Chapter 11
The Threat of Criminal Charges 127
Indecent Exposure Situations 127
The Potential Danger of Accessing Child Pornography 127

Chapter 12
When a Residential Placement May Be Warranted 131

Chapter 13
Preparing for the Transition to Adulthood—The Main Event 135

Chapter 14
Confronting Bullying and Discrimination in the Workplace 147

Chapter 15
Guardianship, Special Needs Trusts, and Powers of Attorney 153

Chapter 16
The Advent of Telehealth Instruction During The COVID-19 Pandemic 157

Chapter 17
The Road Ahead—Institutionalizing High Expectations and Discontent 163

PART II – Advice From the Experts ....

Appendix A 169
Teaching Generalization For a More Independent and Enriched Life

By Dr. Amy Davies-Lackey, BCBA, LBA

Appendix B 175
Observing and Assessing Mainstream, Inclusion, and Special Education Classrooms—What I Look For

By David Salsberg, Psy.D.

Appendix C 185
Using Assessments and Evaluations to Develop a Reasonably Calculated and Appropriately Ambitious IEP

By Jennifer Oratio, Ph.D.

Appendix D 205
Evaluating Speech and Language Needs with the Right Assessment Tools

By Dr. Steven Blaustein, CCC-SLP

Appendix E 213
Bullying Tips for Parents: Q & A with Michael Dreiblatt of Nonprofit STAND UP to Bullying

STAND UP to Bullying

Introduction—Welcome To The Age Of Uncertainty

The world of autism has become far more challenging and complex since the release of my 2004 field guide for parents, *How to Compromise with Your School District Without Compromising Your Child*. Today, 1 in 54 children will be diagnosed on the autism spectrum. Each year in the United States alone, more than 50,000 individuals with autism will transition to adulthood only to face the likely prospect of unemployment, the abrupt end of their educational entitlements, and limited housing and program options that can vary wildly from state to state. Of course, as if affected families did not already have enough on their plate, the entire world is attempting to tame an unseen threat to health and public safety. No one on the planet is exempt from the pervasive uncertainty that defines this difficult time.

A few weeks before this book was ready to go to print, the COVID-19 pandemic arrived in full fury, changing our everyday lives overnight. The entire country was thrust headlong into lockdown and social distance mode. Tens of millions of Americans lost their jobs or livelihoods. The nation's schools were summarily closed, forcing public and private schools alike to send millions of students home indefinitely where the only option was for these students to access remote teaching technology, with their parents or other caregivers trying their level best to act as effective teacher surrogates.

We know that with highly individualized teaching and related support, today's students with autism can learn a great deal and go further than ever before. One thing we have learned about remote teaching technology, however, is that it's <u>not</u> about attendance—it's much more about *attending*. While remote teaching may not be ideal as a core, "across the board" teaching methodology, as a practical matter, it is here to stay in one form or another and it is likely to have particular utility and value in the context of parent training, transition support and social skills development. (*See* Chapter 16)

Even today, no one knows for sure when the nation's schools will actually reopen. That issue is being decided on a state-by-state basis. As at the very beginning of May, 2020, most public and private schools were still formulating plans to open in time for the start of the 2020-2021 school year. By mid-May, however, ongoing concerns over safety forced a painful reconsideration of those plans. The absolute last thing that any school would want is to inadvertently become an incubator for yet another outbreak. Some schools across the country are already communicating or at least telegraphing that the return to school in September, 2020 will be virtual, or at least largely so.

The real issue, however, has nothing to do with setting a date on the calendar for a return to the classroom. The real question is what school will *look* like when students walk through the schoolhouse door given the serious ongoing concerns about public safety. Will there be temperature checks when students enter their school building? Likely. Will students and staff be required to wear masks? Also very likely. How will class size and student-to-teacher ratios be reconciled with concerns over safety and public health? This is yet to be determined. Will the fact that private schools normally feature significantly smaller (and thus safer) class sizes make it any easier for parents to settle their due process cases? I'm thinking "yes."

Will classrooms, lunchrooms, assemblies and test-taking venues need to be reconfigured to maintain a specified physical distance between students and staff? You can bet on it. "How" always is the real uncertainty. How, for example, will related services be provided? How should a school respond if a student or staff member at a reopened school tests positive for COVID-19? To what extent will the protocols of dealing with the threat of COVID-19 (e.g. frequent and thorough hand washing) impact on teaching safe hygiene and other activities of daily living? What will happen to sports programs and other extracurricular activities that involve a level of physical contact? How will COVID-19 impact "the right of students to be educated in the "least restrictive environment?" How will bus transportation be affected? The playbook for these issues and others has yet to be written. Parents and school systems will need to adapt and innovate as needed.[1]

The pandemic arrived as an existential threat to public health and safety. In turn, the nation's *reaction* to the pandemic gave rise to a serious civil rights threat. Buried within the $2.2 trillion dollar CARES Act economic stimulus package enacted in March, 2020 was a provision requiring the Secretary of Education, Betsy DeVos, to identify portions of the federal IDEA statute that, in the opinion of the Secretary, are provisions that Congress should "waive."

I'm not at liberty to disclose everything that my law firm did in an effort to neutralize this serious threat. I can say, however, that we did our part and that on April 27, 2020, we all breathed a collective sigh of relief when Secretary DeVos delivered a letter to ranking members of Congress in which she made clear that she is not requesting waiver authority for any of IDEA's "core tenets." Thankfully, the few waivers being sought by Secretary DeVos will not have any impact on the right to a "free and appropriate public education" (FAPE).

Preserving IDEA's mandates and protections in the face of the pandemic and its resulting economic and other consequences was absolutely essential because in 2017, a unanimous Supreme Court clarified the statutory right to a "free and appropriate public

---

[1] At least one school I have spoken with recently is planning on sending teachers into the student's home periodically to reinforce the student's remote teaching program.

education" (FAPE) as being markedly more robust and ambitious than a number of federal circuit courts had ruled during the prior 35 years. Protected by this new national standard of care, we finally had opened up a window of opportunity to empower the next generations by creating options that can add measurably to the quality of life. Had Secretary DeVos gone further with her waiver recommendations, Congress could easily have materially diluted or even nullified the Supreme Court's new national FAPE standard. Whatever the future may bring, we can never take these essential statutory protections for granted.

While an understanding of the law and the applicable statutes is important, the primary focus of *Autism's Declaration of Independence* is substance and practicality, with a constant eye on the ultimate outcome. Pretty much any student can "graduate" *from* the public education system. However, what steps can be taken to make sure that a student with the potential to do so has sufficiently acquired the functional skills for graduating *to* something that is personally meaningful and fulfilling for them? The transition to adulthood when IDEA's educational entitlements come to an end is, of course, the "main event." (See Chapter 13)

From the start of the student's assessment process to the graduation ceremony, what is the plan to develop greater levels of independence and self-sufficiency? The pandemic has shown us just how volatile and unforgiving life can be. What may be here today might well be gone tomorrow. No parent can live forever and there are so few institutions and other things we can genuinely rely upon. In this age of uncertainty, how, then, should parents advocate and access funding for the services, school placements, and "transition" programming their child will require to achieve a good outcome after exiting the public education system? How can we make it easier for families to navigate the many systems that they will encounter? What is the significance of maintaining high expectations? How should parents go about developing and shaping a plan for the future in the context of this new and difficult era? These are some of the questions I have attempted to address in this book.

Two decades ago, I left a lucrative law partnership in Manhattan to found the nation's first law firm dedicated to the representation of individuals with autism. If there ever was a niche law practice, this would be it. I've been incredibly fortunate to have had the opportunity to work with hundreds of autism professionals and more than a thousand families across 35 states. I love doing what I do.

From the vantage point of my experience, I urge that a student's available options and choices upon the student's transition to adulthood will turn on the student's ability to generalize and sustain learning in a safe environment, coupled with the quality, integrity, and effectiveness of the student's pre-transition educational experience, all put into motion by high expectations and the effective advocacy that is essential to individualizing the learning experience. The strategies contained in *Autism's Declaration of Independence* are designed to help parents and professionals harness these many moving pieces, understanding that each child's potential and needs are unique.

There are many books written on autism from a clinical perspective. There also are the "these are your legal rights" guides that focus on the applicable legal standards. *Autism's Declaration of Independence* aims to reconcile both of these inextricably intertwined perspectives in the context of these difficult times, while providing many useful and practical tips along the way.

In Part II, contributions from some of the most experienced professionals in the field provide invaluable insight that parents and professionals can turn to again and again. These appendices explain the assessment process and generalization—how important it is to build a solid foundation based upon an individual's unique needs and learning process. Last but not least, the final appendix addresses the serious national problem of bullying.

I've also included vignettes from many actual client experiences. Elopement from school. The threat of sexual abuse in a public-school setting. Fighting for Applied Behavior Analysis (ABA) programming in Tennessee. Bullying in the classroom and, later, bullying in the workplace. The dangers associated with police encounters. The challenge of educating a child with autism in a remote section of the country. The challenge of remote learning at home and the related challenge of practicing "social distance" for a population that normally spends so much of its time trying to learn how to *bridge* social distance. Dealing with disciplinary matters. Preparing for school lockdown drills where the threat being prepared for is an active shooter. Advocating for access to extracurricular sports activities—and more.

Whatever the issue at hand, my objective is that these compelling case studies and personal accounts will help bring the subject matter to life for the reader, providing just a little more certainty and predictability to help families and professionals navigate these difficult and uncertain times. My ultimate hope is that the information, resources and strategies contained in *Autism's Declaration of Independence* will help the next generation achieve the best possible outcome.

About the Author

Gary Mayerson graduated from the Georgetown University Law Center and the S.I. Newhouse School of Public Communications at Syracuse University.

In 2000, after representing high-profile litigation clients including Donald Trump and former Beatle George Harrison, Gary withdrew from a lucrative Manhattan law partnership to found Mayerson & Associates (www.mayerslaw.com) as the nation's first civil rights law firm dedicated to the representation of individuals with autism. Gary was inspired to start his highly specialized firm after a family member was diagnosed with autism and he saw firsthand how difficult it can be for parents to obtain effective programs and services.

To date, Gary and his colleagues have represented more than 1200 autism families in 35 states, including Alaska. Gary also consults to expatriate and other families living abroad who are in the process of relocating to the United States. Gary and his firm are responsible for more than 150 important federal court decisions hailing from the Second, Third, Fifth, Sixth, Tenth, and Eleventh Circuits—as well as *Deal v. Hamilton County Department of Education*, the first autism case to reach the U.S. Supreme Court.

One of Gary's federal court decisions, *T.K. v. NYCDOE*, is widely considered to be a landmark ruling responding to the important problem of bullying. In *Doe v. Darien*, despite the absence of any eyewitnesses or physical evidence, Gary and his litigation team proved to the satisfaction of a federal jury in New Haven, Connecticut, that a 12-year-old public school student with serious communication challenges had, in fact, been sexually abused by his paraprofessional. The jury's verdict in *Doe v. Darien* confirms an incredibly important principle: that a student with a disability has the same right as any other student to have his or her words respected.

In *Ermini v. Vittori*, an international custodial dispute arising under the Hague Convention, Gary and the amicus brief he submitted on behalf of Autism Speaks helped persuade the Second Circuit Court of Appeals to allow a young Italian boy with autism to remain in the U.S., as his mother wished, so that he could receive essential therapy not then available in Italy. In the *Starego* case, after a high-school student with autism had aged out of his varsity eligibility, Gary was able to extend that student's eligibility to remain a placekicker for his high school football team—which went on that year to win the state championship.

Gary and his law firm served as amicus counsel for Autism Speaks in connection with the Supreme Court's defining 2017 decision in *Endrew F.* In March 2019, New York Law School published Gary's law review article, *Generalization After Endrew F.* Gary makes the compelling case that in light of the Supreme Court's robust ruling in *Endrew F.*, the federal courts should finally embrace the generalization process as the critical catalyst and "secret sauce" needed to produce greater levels of independence.

Gary has testified before Congress and has been interviewed by CNN, NPR, Katie Couric, Dan Rather, the *Washington Post*, the *New York Times*, the *Boston Globe*, the *Wall Street* Journal, *The Economist*, and *The Atlantic*. He has presented at the United Nations, Teacher's College (Columbia University), Yale University's Department of Psychiatry, Yale University's Child Study Team, New York University Hospital, New York Law School, Northeastern University Law School, the Manhattan corporate headquarters of American Express, the Manhattan headquarters of Wells Fargo, and the Vermont Statehouse.

Acknowledgements

Many people deserve thanks for contributing to this book. Some, unfortunately, are no longer with us. At the risk of forgetting someone, I'd like to thank the late Keith Amersen, Julie Azuma, Jean Marie Brescia, Steven Blaustein, Gary Brill, Shirley Cohen, Eustacia Cutler, Amy Davies-Lackey, Sara Daum, Philip and Maureen Deal, Melissa DiPeri, Jacqueline DeVore, Michael Dreiblatt, James D'Auguste, Orrin Devinsky, Ivy Feldman, Dena Gassner, Joanne Gerenser, Emily Gerson-Saines, Lisa Goring, Temple Grandin, the late Fadi Haddad, Sara Kahn, Allison Kleinman, Ami Klin, Amy Davies-Lackey, the late O. Ivar Lovaas, Nina Lovaas, Richard Marsico, Lilli Mayerson, Cece McCarton, Tina McCourt, Maria McGinley, John McEachin, James Mulick, Jennifer Oratio, Judy Palazzo, Judy Pletnikoff, Katje Richstatter, the late Todd Risley, Fredda Rosen, David Salsberg, Steven Shore, Shirley Silver, Alison Singer, the Starego family, Vincent Strully, Fred Volkmar, Alexander Westphal, Janet Wolfe, Bob Wright, and the late Suzanne Wright.

A Note on Client Confidentiality

Confidentiality and the attorney-client privilege is at the heart of every attorney-client relationship. Except in those few cases where "name" confidentiality was expressly waived by the client family, the case vignettes and client references you are about to read have all been edited to protect and preserve the clients' identities.

In some instances, it was sufficient to substitute initials in the place of surnames. In others, it was necessary to change gender, geography, or some other inconsequential detail. The "Doe" family listed as the plaintiffs in *Doe v. Darien* is a surname pseudonym approved and adopted by the federal district court to protect the family's privacy. In the remaining references where actual client surnames appear, unless the client's identity already was a matter of public record, the client family either authorized the disclosure or specifically requested, in the public interest, that their surname be used.

PART I

Knowing Your Child's Rights and How to Apply Them

Chapter 1
The Autism Diagnosis and Its Impact on the Family

Few moments in time will have a more profound and devastating impact for a family than the moment when parents are told that their beautiful child meets criteria for an autism diagnosis. As former boxing heavyweight champion Mike Tyson once remarked, "Everyone has a plan until they get punched in the face." For many parents, receiving the diagnosis of autism is a lot like being punched in the face *by* Mike Tyson. Now what?[2]

Usually, the parents' pre-diagnosis plan includes high hopes of academic and related achievement over time and belief in an ultimate outcome that, at the very least, involves their child developing into a happy, safe, employable, and self-sufficient adult. After an autism diagnosis, those dreams and high expectations can come to a crashing halt, morphing into a pall of fear, anxiety and uncertainty. Overnight, everything has changed.

This is the moment when parents resolve to become more informed and get help. They start calling agencies, organizations, evaluators, schools, therapists, and family members. They scour the Internet for articles, books, and blogs. They contact other parents. At about this time, many parents realize that they are receiving quite a bit of conflicting advice from a variety of sources.[3] With all the conflicting advice, how are parents to make the many important decisions that are needed?

The parent, now a card-carrying member of a club they never intended to join, is probably confronting a litany of questions that will have no immediate or reliable answers: Will my child ever learn to speak or at least develop a functional system of

---

2 Parents will ask themselves the very same question that Captain Chesley ("Sully") Sullenberger had only seconds to resolve on January 15, 2009, when a flock of Canadian geese struck and disabled US Airways Flight 1549 ("How am I ever going to land this plane?").
3 Given that every child with autism is unique, this is to be expected.

communication? Will my child be employable? Will my child be able to enter into and sustain a relationship? Will they have any friends? Will they ever have children of their own? Will they be happy and safe? How will this diagnosis impact our family dynamic? Will my child be able to drive? Is going to college a possibility? Will my child ever be able to live on their own? What kind of school or program does my child need right now? Can my child's educational needs be addressed and met within the public school system? Who are the professionals I need to consult with now so that I have the best chance of making the right decisions?

Former presidential candidate Andrew Yang likes to say that the fact that so many people today either know someone or have a family member with autism is part of the "new normal." If the "new normal" for your family means now having to go to Plan B, what is Plan B going to look like and how much is it all going to cost? How am I supposed to implement *any* plan smack in the middle of a pandemic? What happens when I'm dead and gone? There is no end to the real and serious concerns that keep parents up at night, staring at the ceiling. I know that ceiling well.

Are We Really Seeing an Autism "Tsunami?"

Just three decades ago, the incidence rate of autism was reported to be approximately 2 in 10,000. Today, the incidence rate reported by the National Institutes of Health is a staggering 1 in 54. A study from South Korea is even more alarming—1 in 38. Some commentators speak of an "autism tsunami" of epic proportions caused by a confluence of genetic factors and environmental triggers. Others conclude that the current statistics are simply the byproduct of better diagnostics, greater public awareness, and the recognition that, just as there are multiple variants of cancer, the autism spectrum involves multiple subtypes as well. The ongoing scientific debate on this point is not likely to be resolved anytime soon.

No matter. Once autism lands in your own backyard and your family becomes part of autism's statistical database, spreading autism awareness and debating the accuracy of autism's reported incidence rate will probably take a second seat to more practical and immediate concerns. For children already in the here and now, who struggle to learn skills that most neurotypical peers will easily pick up simply by watching other children do them, the burning question is not where the autism came from. Rather, the critical issue is devising and implementing demonstrably effective intervention and teaching strategies that, over time, are designed and "reasonably calculated" to promote ever-increasing levels of independence and self-sufficiency. This necessarily entails pursuing an outcome oriented, data-driven approach, much like the way successful corporations measure and track their progress achieving strategic and financial goals.

Obstacle Courses Parents Will Need to Navigate

If you are a parent being inundated with all kinds of unsolicited advice from every quarter, it can be difficult to know where and how to begin the search for effective services. As discussed in Part II (page 167), choosing the right mix of baseline evaluations and assessments requires careful decision-making. To compound matters, the process of securing services and programming comes with highly specialized terminology and acronyms. Even worse, this terminology can differ from state to state. It is especially frustrating that in a relatively brief time frame, parents are forced to navigate between several distinct entitlement systems that are each extremely time-sensitive.

While early intervention programming (birth to 3 years) is available in each state pursuant to an Individualized Family Services Plan (IFSP), before you know it, your child is "aging out" of early intervention and must now be processed through the preschool (3–5 years) system.[4] Even the preschool time frame is limited, as parents must then look forward to preparing for and attending the "turning 5" meeting that will develop the student's school-age Individualized Education Plan (IEP).

Winning a relay race depends on smooth transitions and handoffs. If not properly managed and planned for, the transitional overlaps between the above systems can put a student in educational limbo—the very last thing that a student on the spectrum needs.

Years later, in what seems like the blink of an eye, your student exits the public educational system and "graduates" to adulthood. That shift, commonly referred to as "going off the services cliff," moves the student from a program of enforceable educational *entitlements* to a program of *eligibility* and long waiting lists.

The Special Language Used in the Land of Special Education

The Individuals with Disabilities Education Act (IDEA) is the controlling federal statute. The statutory scheme is one that allows states to do *better*, but not worse, than what the federal statute mandates. For example, while the federal IDEA statute requires "transition" supports to be implemented in earnest by the time a student turns 16, New York State makes the trigger age 15. The State of Connecticut has an even more generous statute, making the trigger age 14. There is consensus that the earlier a student starts the

---

4 At the time this book is going to print, in response to the many disruptions caused by the COVID-19 pandemic, Secretary of Education Betsy DeVos is seeking limited "timeline" waivers from Congress that, if implemented, will have the effect of temporarily *extending* early intervention services past a toddler's third birthday.

transition process, the better the outcome is likely to be.

Each state maintains its own acronyms and terminology for the process of developing a student's Individualized Education Plan (IEP), the recognized "centerpiece" of every special education program. In Texas, for example, the IEP meeting is referred to as an ARD (admission, review, and dismissal). Connecticut, on the other hand, has its PPT (planning and placement team) meeting. In New Jersey, parents receive notice to attend a meeting of the CST (child study team). Supreme Court Justice Samuel Alito aptly referred to this highly specialized language as a "blizzard of words." Unfortunately, they don't teach you about the special education "blizzard" in most law schools.

Preventing or Neutralizing Disagreement with Quality Evaluations

The student's available options during his or her transition to adulthood are very much impacted by the extent that the student was able to identify, access, and enforce their educational entitlements *before* exiting the educational system. The fact that educational rights are *enforceable* does not necessarily mean that the rights in question are actually being observed and enforced.

Such is the difference between virtual reality and reality-reality. In this connection, a child's entitlements during the public-school timeframe are directly related to how successful parents and their advocates are in demonstrating the child's unique needs. Conflicts will arise when, for example, the school district disagrees with parents concerning the existence and severity of the child's needs. Accordingly, often the best course of action is taking steps to *preempt* the opportunity for disagreement.

In the first instance, the ability to advocate for a child's needs normally will turn on the quality and persuasiveness of the information and recommendations appearing in a child's assessments. The Appendices to this book (page 169), graciously contributed by Dr. Amy Davies-Lackey, Dr. Jennifer Oratio, Dr. Steven Blaustein, and Dr. David Salsberg, offer a comprehensive overview of the numerous assessment tools and measures that are available—as well as some important factors that parents and professionals should be looking for when observing, considering, and assessing the appropriateness of school placements. Quality, highly individualized assessments are often the key to getting off to a good start and making a good record. These assessments normally need to be timely shared with the local school district or early intervention program. They are of little value if squirreled away in a desk drawer or filing cabinet.

Conflict with the School District Is Often Avoidable

Every child with a disability needs an effective and informed advocate. The need for effective advocacy does not mean, however, that conflict with the school district is inevitable. The pioneering work of earlier families in the federal court process has paved much of the way for today's families, so that they need not always "reinvent the wheel." Today, many parents and school districts are able to anticipate and collaboratively work out issues *before* they devolve into contentious disputes. The best dispute is the one that you don't have to litigate.

Unfortunately, not all disagreements can be resolved. Conflicts will often arise during or after the "turning five" process. In many states, this is precisely when the school district begins to assume a much greater role and responsibility in *funding* the student's program. It is amazing how many services that appear on the student's preschool IEP will be deemed unnecessary by the school district when it is required to pay for those services. With large budget deficits running in the background, we can expect to see more and more school districts holding the line during the "turning five" process. Yet another reason for parents to secure quality evaluations that will help make a good record.

Why Promoting Greater Independence Before Adulthood Is Critical

The available data tells us why it is essential to carefully focus our educational energy so students on the autism spectrum who graduate from the public education system will emerge with greater levels of independence and self-sufficiency.

We know that each year, more than 50,000 students with autism will transition to adulthood. We also know that when students with autism graduate from and age out of the public education system, they will face a daunting 85% unemployment rate at a time when the neurotypical population is being challenged with an unemployment rate presently closer to 20%.[5] Finally, we know that because of what has become a nationwide housing crisis affecting adults with autism, many of these young, mostly unemployed adults are likely to live with their parents for a long time. That is, until they can't.

Many parents may want to "live forever" to protect their children long after they have transitioned to adulthood; these parents know, however, that living forever is not a viable plan for the future. I don't mean to be cold or harsh, but one day we will all be facing a more permanent metaphysical transition. Nor is it realistic for parents to assume that they will not encounter health issues interfering with or even precluding performance of the parental role. A parent does not have to test positive for COVID-19 to be out of commission. Even the recuperation period following an unanticipated ankle sprain can

---

5 The unemployment rate during the Great Depression was approximately 24%. This provides some perspective as to the impact of the 85% unemployment rate that people with disabilities face.

wreak havoc.

Accordingly, in the limited time that parents have to be parents—and in the limited time that students are entitled to services and supports from the public school system—it is imperative that parents advocate for and pursue educational programs that are "reasonably calculated" to promote and generalize greater levels of independence. In this connection, it is essential that our legislators, the judiciary, and the educational community recognize the pursuit of greater levels of independence and self-sufficiency as the national priority that it is.

Independence and self-sufficiency, however, does not mean learning how to become a self-reliant hermit. Ironically, to become more independent, one must learn how to access, manage, and take advantage of the many social and business connections that are needed to make life in a society work.

The Autism "Refugee Crisis"

Many parents of newly diagnosed children will quickly discover that services available in states such as Massachusetts, California, New York, Connecticut, or New Jersey may not be accessible in states such as Alabama, Louisiana, North Dakota, or West Virginia. The same holds true for most students living in remote communities. In general, states that spend more money per pupil to educate their neurotypical population can be expected to offer better programs to special needs students.[6] This disparity in the availability of resources has spawned a refugee crisis of sorts: far too many American families are having to pick up their lives to move to states and communities thought to offer quality special education services. The state-by-state disparity in resources may improve somewhat over the next decade, but for now, newly diagnosed families often still need to call for the moving van to seek out a more hospitable and generous state.[7]

The COVID-19 pandemic has also forced many families to reconsider their current living arrangements, particularly if those families are living in congested high-rise apartment buildings or are taking the subway or other forms of public transportation where maintaining a safe social distance may be difficult, if not impossible. At least until an effective vaccine can be developed, more and more families presently living and working in congested urban areas will be giving serious thought to moving to far less congested environments. Safety and health is and will continue to be number one.

---

6 For example, while Louisiana spends roughly $11,000 per year to educate its neurotypical students, New Jersey spends a whopping $18,000 per pupil.

7 Sometimes, more than a moving van is required. Over the years, we have represented many "expats" and other families returning or moving to the U.S. from Hong Kong, London, Cairo, Tel Aviv, Mumbai, Paris, and Tokyo.

Accordingly, at least for some parents, that house in the suburbs is starting to look more and more attractive. The tradeoff is that a suburban school district normally will want a child attending its autism program.

Autism "Acceptance" Goes Only So Far

Today, traditional advocacy is being complemented by inspired self-advocacy. The level of self-advocacy we see today would have been unthinkable just a generation ago. In general, the rise in self-advocacy is a positive and welcome development. But, as autism covers a broad spectrum, we must never lose sight of the fact that an outspoken branch of the self-advocacy movement's singular focus on societal "acceptance" offers inadequate protection for those individuals in the autism population whose severity, communication, or behavioral challenges cry out for support and intervention.

Social acceptance is an important objective: of course people on the spectrum should be accepted and included! However, it should not be controversial or considered patronizing to take the position that the most vulnerable among us need a great deal of targeted help and therapeutic support *beyond* acceptance. At the end of the day, it is important not to follow someone else's vision of political correctness down the rabbit hole: we need to face facts. There is no limit to what some individuals on the spectrum can accomplish. On the other hand, providing therapeutic or guardianship support to those who clearly need it is a moral and ethical responsibility none of us can afford to ignore under the banner of "neurodiversity."

I'm not a neuropsychologist, behavior analyst or speech therapist. I'm a civil rights lawyer, as well as a parent. However, over the years, I've had the unique opportunity to work with well over a thousand affected families and hundreds of talented professionals. If I have learned anything, it's that every child is unique and the path to a successful outcome is not linear.

Pursuing a good outcome[8] requires more than a singular grand battle plan. Having and sustaining high expectations is a must. While civility is important, when a child's future is at stake, we cannot afford to walk on eggshells while working with the local school system. We must be direct and not afraid to express frustration and

---

8   When I speak of achieving a good outcome, I necessarily am speaking about what would be considered a good outcome for that particular student, with their unique strengths, challenges, and potential. This is important to bear in mind, as parents and professionals devote significant energy attempting to shrink the "gap" in functioning between children with autism and their neurotypical peers. Even if a child ultimately is placed in a residential setting, the objective might be to have that child arrive at that placement with a higher level of independence and self-sufficiency. As Baseball Hall of Famer Carlton Fisk remarked, "It's not what you achieve, but rather what you *overcome*."

dissatisfaction. Moreover, parents constantly need to regroup and modify the approach based on the child's demonstrable progress. For a number of parents, being in pursuit of a good outcome can feel like a 24/7 full-court press. And often, that's exactly what it is.[9]

Every child's unique needs will change over time. The pursuit of a good outcome is a *shaping* process, entailing a series of individualized plans keenly attuned to the student's evolving needs, as well as access to trained, talented professionals who are ready, willing, and able to implement those plans. This is a lot easier said than done! Sometimes, you will take two steps forward only to take two steps back. And, when it becomes apparent that your well-conceived plan is not working as anticipated, it is essential to quickly identify and change the components standing in the way of progress.

Sometimes, this process means going back to the drawing board. Sometimes it means getting an entirely new drawing board—or you realize you need several boards because there are so many moving pieces. No matter how good a plan may look "on paper," no one should remain stubbornly tethered to a plan that, despite everyone's diligent efforts, is not working. Just as is the case on Wall Street, it is important to know when to sell.[10]

How To Weigh the Non-Financial Costs

Whether you are looking at a choice in programming through the lens of the parent or school district, it is important to bear in mind that every intervention or teaching opportunity comes with its own non-financial "cost." For the student receiving an hour of counseling from the school guidance counselor, the "cost" is the time that could have been spent working on *other* needs and skill sets that might be more valuable for the student's progress. What good is memorizing a series of scientific formulas if the student does not have a functional system of communication? The same "cost" concerns arise when a student is spending hours practicing skills that have been demonstrably mastered, or that are of questionable relevance.[11]

---

9   Most parents that I see employing a relentless, 24/7 approach fall into two categories: The first involves students whose severity is palpable and pervasive across all domains; the second involves students who have a great deal of potential and who are "on the fence."

10 It also is important to know when to stay the course, recognizing that even the most successful of programs will include moments when the student *appears* to be taking a few steps backward. A good example of this is the phenomenon of the "extinction burst," where the data may be showing an *increase* in the frequency and duration of an interfering behavior just before the target behavior is about to be extinguished. The data might provide the temptation to change course when, in actuality, change is the last thing that is warranted.

11 For example, it is a complete waste of a student's precious learning time to learn the day Mother's Day falls on the calendar because that date changes from year to year. It also is not efficient to spend a lot of time

Similarly, if a student with autism is being educated and supported in a mainstream classroom, it can cost the student dearly when being constantly "pulled out" of the orbit of his or her classroom to work with a related service provider in another part of the school. At some point, it can be far more effective to provide services on a "push in" basis or provide the services after school, allowing the student more time to learn, socialize, and communicate with classroom peers.

Parents and school districts need to give this non-financial cost factor serious consideration, recognizing that autism is a relentless workaholic and that every hour of teaching time is a precious opportunity that cannot be squandered. This means constantly reexamining *what* we are teaching every bit as much as how and when we are teaching. When, for example, the COVID-19 pandemic forced public and private schools to transition to remote teaching, teachers and administrators were forced to prioritize, if not triage, the matters that a student would be encountering and working with on a computer screen.

An additional potential "cost" might be the potential health risk to a student or his or her parents if, for example, a student is being asked to participate in a currently risky and unsafe activity that previously was not thought to come with any health or safety concerns (e.g. "Hey class—who wants to play 'Twister'?")

Keeping Classic Academics in Its Proper Perspective

Well-intentioned educational programs can inadvertently waste a great deal of teaching time that could be put to better use. While classic academics certainly occupy a valuable position in the educational arsenal (particularly for students who will go on to a college experience), a search engine can instantaneously tell you when the Battle of Hastings took place, the names of all the U.S. presidents, or a basic explanation of Einstein's theory of relativity. No wonder, then, that smartphones are prohibited during final exams!

From my vantage point, the reason so much of the adult autism population is unemployed (or underemployed) has very little to do with classic academic achievement and much more with the extent of a student's behavioral, communication, and social challenges—not to mention whether the student has received adequate training in skill sets that are useful and valuable to employers. For many students, it is far more important for them to acquire solid social skills than it is to attend an advanced placement math class.

Today, more students with autism than ever before will go on to college, graduate

---

working on what the student has already solidly mastered.

school, or another post-secondary experience. Still, most will *not* have that opportunity. While classic academics will continue to have their place, school systems are obligated to offer well-coordinated vocational and related "transition" programs for students on the autism spectrum so they might acquire the skills needed to land a sustainable, paying job after graduation.

This is not a matter of debate. As discussed in Chapter 13 (page 135), transition-related programming is an extremely important statutory mandate that applies in all 50 states and in every public-school district. Parents need to take full advantage of this mandate long before their child gets ready to leave the public-school system. A student's graduation ceremony is not the culmination; it should represent the beginning of the next chapter. Transition-related programming is the vehicle that is supposed to prepare students for that next chapter. In chapter 13, I will explain how the remote teaching technology that was implemented in response to the COVID-19 lockdown can be leveraged to help energize and support the transition process.

With Ivar and Nina Lovaas In Los Angeles

Two Early Lawsuits Regarding the Efficacy of ABA Interventions

As noted earlier, today's families have been spared many of the earlier conflicts parents were forced to slog through with no assurance that they would prevail. In the early years of my law firm, we were forced to file lawsuit after lawsuit to establish the efficacy and legitimacy of Applied Behavior Analysis (ABA) as a scientifically validated teaching methodology and autism intervention.

We had to reinvent that wheel time and again. Many school districts woodenly resisted ABA programs (then often referred to generically as "Lovaas Therapy")[12]

---

12 I owe much to the late Dr. Ivar Lovaas and his accomplished wife Nina. While Dr. Lovaas and his colleagues at UCLA did not invent the field of Applied Behavior Analysis (ABA), they are well known for their 1987 and

because they feared "opening the floodgates"; because school personnel had little training or experience implementing ABA; or because ABA was regarded as some kind of wacky cult.[13] Two cases—involving the Pletnikoff family in Alaska and the Deal family in Tennessee—represent two very different examples of ABA advocacy and the unique lessons learned.

Kodiak Island, Alaska and the *Pletnikoff* Case

In 1998, I traveled to Kodiak Island, Alaska, to advocate on behalf of Nick Pletnikoff, a young boy with autism who was making excellent progress in an ABA program that his family had assembled and his school district was reluctant to support. In 1998, it often was a struggle to put together an effective ABA program, even for parents who lived in densely populated cities like New York, Chicago, or Los Angeles. Somehow, Nick's family had managed to create an excellent ABA program on a relatively remote island where there are almost as many brown bears as people.[14] The "big picture" was my belief that if we could persuade remote, resource-challenged school districts such as Kodiak Island to fund and support quality ABA programming, it would make it that much easier to persuade school systems with the resources to do so.

Nick's incredibly smart, resourceful, and relentless mother, Judy, imported Dr. John McEachin from Autism Partnership in Los Angeles, California and Dr. James Mulick from Children's Hospital in Ohio to develop and modify Nick's ABA program. Somehow, Judy and her passion convinced the local order of Catholic nuns to implement and take data on Nick's ABA program. The sisters were highly motivated to help. Their data collection efforts were precise and exacting, if not impeccable. (Those of you who had a Catholic school experience know what I'm talking about.)

Judy and her family had lived on Kodiak Island for many years and hoped to continue. The Pletnikoff family wanted me to vindicate Nick's statutory entitlements

---

1993 studies, published in peer-reviewed journals, proving the efficacy of ABA as a core autism intervention. However, it was their kindness and loving respect for families that stands out most in my mind: They appreciated autism's profound impact on the family. If Ivar and Nina had a mantra, it was "Listen to the parents and always have high expectations."

13 There also was tremendous resistance to ABA because the earliest attempts to teach in an ABA format used "aversives." The science of applied behavior analysis has evolved and changed tremendously over the years. Today's ABA programs rely on positive reinforcement and include "natural environment teaching."

14 With a human population just over 6,000, Kodiak Island also is home to nearly 3,000 brown (Kodiak) bears, making it one of the densest bear populations in the world. Kodiak has its bears much like Manhattan has its pigeons. The Kodiak bear subspecies is the largest brown bear, second in size only to the polar bear. Shortly after arriving on Kodiak, I received detailed instructions from Judy Pletnikoff for "what to do" (and what not to do) when confronting a Kodiak bear. Fortunately, I never had the need to follow Judy's instructions.

and protections without causing offense within their close-knit community. This was a tall order requiring a creative, sensitive approach. I promised Judy and her family that I would make every effort to maintain their relationships within the community, recognizing that preserving goodwill could be critical in avoiding future conflict.

Just before some especially damaging evidence was about to be entered into the record, the school district's attorney approached me about entering into a multiyear settlement that would allow the Pletnikoff family to continue funding Nick's ABA program. Ultimately, I was able to make peace with the Kodiak Island school system without disturbing any of the family's relationships (and without provoking any members of the local bear population). The Pletnikoffs were happy. The school district was happy. Any further disagreements were easily resolved without me having to fly back to Kodiak Island.[15]

Armed with funding from the Kodiak Island school system, Nick made excellent progress in his ABA-based program. Still, Nick's progress was patiently built, brick-by-brick. It took *years* for Nick to learn how to ask for what he wanted, follow directions, respond to questions, and have a meaningful conversation.

Nick attended regular education classes at St. Mary's Elementary School, where he learned to read, write, and do arithmetic alongside the other children of Kodiak. Nick came to be familiar with and appreciated by his neighbors—he became a relatively full participant in community life. With the help of his parents, Nick even learned to operate a small business creating and selling pet identification tags. Over time, Nick was becoming more and more independent. Life was good![16]

---

15 The positive experience I had working collaboratively with the Kodiak Island school system and its counsel inspired me to write my first field guide for parents, *How To Compromise With Your School District Without Compromising Your Child*. I am very much a proponent of compromise. However, there is little room for compromise once harm is threatened. Accordingly, knowing and understanding where harm begins is essential to the settlement process. This is one of the main reasons it is so important for parents to have good assessments and evaluations to rely upon.

16 Nick Pletnikoff's story is also featured in Chapter 9, Managing Safety Considerations (page 95). In 2015, a violent and terrifying physical confrontation with a police officer—behavior that was captured on a police bodycam—caused serious trauma and regression that Nick is still recovering from.

On Kodiak Island with Judy Pletnikoff,
John McEachin, and James Mulick

<u>The Tennessee School District That Spent Over $3 Million Defending the Indefensible</u>

Of course, not every contested autism case goes as smoothly as it did on Kodiak Island. The most difficult and hard-fought case I ever litigated is easily *Zachary Deal v. Hamilton County (Tennessee)*, the very first autism case to reach the U.S. Supreme Court.

In 1999, Zachary's parents (then residents of Chattanooga, Tennessee) approached the Hamilton County Tennessee school system requesting it consider an Applied Behavior Analysis–based program that would provide the one-to-one instruction and behavioral support Zachary needed to learn and attend school. Unfortunately, every time Zachary's parents attempted to bring up the subject of ABA for a meaningful discussion, they were immediately shot down by school district administrators who stubbornly refused to consider their requests.

After the Deal family brought suit, Hamilton County and its lawyers engaged in some highly questionable tactics to keep me and one of Zachary's principal experts, Dr. James Mulick, from coming to Tennessee on Zachary's behalf. First, Hamilton County opposed my relatively routine motion to be admitted *pro hac vice* (so that I could represent Zachary in a Tennessee courtroom).

When that tactic failed, Hamilton County's lawyers filed an ethics grievance against me with the local bar association. My offense? I had posted to our firm's website the below photo of me standing just outside the barbed-wire fence enclosure surrounding Hamilton County's administrative buildings. Hamilton County's ethics complaint was filed before any request to take down the photo. Had Hamilton County simply asked, there would never have been any "ethics" complaint. In any event, I immediately took the photo down from our website while Zachary's case was pending.

AUTISM'S DECLARATION OF INDEPENDENCE · 25

Standing Just Outside Hamilton County's
Administrative Offices

Hamilton County then tried to block Dr. Mulick from giving expert testimony at Zachary's trial on the grounds that Dr. Mulick was licensed as a psychologist in Ohio, but not in Tennessee. The State of Tennessee certainly has its share of good psychologists, but Dr. Mulick, a nationally known autism expert, knew a great deal about the scope and effectiveness of Zachary's program. The trial judge, James Andrews, wisely rejected Hamilton County's bizarre attempt to exclude Dr. Mulick from testifying at Zachary's trial.

Tennessee is the same state where the famous Scopes Monkey Trial took place in 1925, pitting evolution and science against scripture; a criminal trial in which Tennessee's Butler Act had made it illegal for a public-school teacher to teach human evolution. Zachary's case was a civil case presenting different issues, but it was not lost on me that, once again, science was on trial; this time, the science of Applied Behavior Analysis.

Zachary's trial went on for three weeks, with Hamilton County objecting to pretty much everything. Every night, the Deals and I and would hunker down in the family's basement "war room" to prepare for the next day's witnesses. Around 10 p.m., after the last round of homemade sweet tea and Jack Daniels was served, someone would drive me to my hotel so I could get some sleep before the next day's proceedings.

The annual cost of Zachary's ABA program was approximately $65,000. At the time, Phil Deal was working as a fundraiser for St. Jude Hospital and Maureen Deal (formerly employed by the FBI as a computer expert who accompanied other FBI agents on raids) was staying at home to manage Zachary's program. It would be difficult to find a family more organized and with more integrity than the Deals.

For the Deals and their modest annual income, the cost of Zachary's program was a real hardship. The last thing the Deals wanted was a knock-down, drag-out court battle.

Rather than work with Zachary's parents toward a compromise that would conserve taxpayer dollars, the Hamilton County school board and its then-Superintendent, Jesse Register, spent more than $3 million in attorneys' and expert witness fees to fight Zachary and his parents during a month-long trial in Chattanooga and litigating the appeals that followed at the federal level. So many families could have been helped with that money.

When a school system invests more than $3 million fighting a single court case over a single child, it is likely banking on the presumption that such tactics will eventually wear down a family with fewer resources to the point where they will give up. That kind of school system is also looking to set an example so that other families will not dare do the same. But Hamilton County did not know who they were dealing with. There were many dark moments when any family might have decided to call it quits. Not the Deals—they were committed to seeing Zachary's case through to the end. The Deals and their commitment and fortitude inspired me and many other families.

Using words such as "appalling," "evasive," and "untruthful," the judge presiding over the *Deal* trial (Hon. James Andrews) ruled for Zachary and his parents in a scathing decision that exposed Hamilton County's shabby and disrespectful treatment. Hamilton County refused to accept any responsibility for its actions and prepared for an appeal siege in which it hired *four* additional, handsomely paid "experts" who had never testified at the trial and had no prior involvement with Zachary's program. People will sometimes ask me how the Hamilton County school system managed to spend millions in legal fees defending a single case. This is how. Hamilton County then doubled down by taking an appeal to federal court. In this way, Hamilton County was able to defer and deflect any accountability for what had happened following the trial. Hamilton County could respond "Oh, that case? It's on appeal."

Judge Edgar, the Chattanooga-based federal district court judge assigned to the case following the school district's appeal, apparently wasn't all that impressed with Judge Andrews' decision in Zachary's favor. Judge Edgar allowed Hamilton County the opportunity to bolster their record with more "expert" testimony from the four additional experts Hamilton County had hired. In essence, Judge Edgar gave Hamilton County the opportunity for a "do-over." Judge Edgar had the power and discretion to do this—there was absolutely nothing that we could do but go along for the ride.

It hardly was a surprise that when the "do-over" phase was completed, Judge Edgar ruled that Hamilton County had done nothing wrong and that there were no procedural or substantive violations. However, on the further appeal filed by the Deals, the Sixth Circuit Court of Appeals ruled otherwise, holding that Hamilton County came into the

IEP process with a "closed mind" and had impermissibly "predetermined" Zachary Deal's educational program by refusing to give any consideration to the Deals' request for ABA teaching. In essence, the appeals court agreed with Judge Andrews' original decision. By the time the *Deal* case wound its way through the federal court system and all the appeals and attempted appeals,[17] Hamilton County emerged (once again) as the losing party after spending a fortune trying to defend the indefensible.

With Phil and Maureen Deal After Oral Argument Before The 6th Circuit

Inasmuch as Zachary emerged from this saga as the prevailing party, Hamilton County was ordered to pay a substantial portion of Zachary's attorneys' fees on top of the millions of dollars it had already paid to its own attorneys and experts.[18] To say the least, Hamilton County could have lost for less—a lot less.

The *Deal* case offers a textbook example of what a school district should *not* do when parents ask to have a meaningful discussion. It also reveals the shameful ordeal that some school districts are capable of putting parents through when disputes arise. I am especially proud that in her dissenting opinion in *Schaffer v. Weast*,[19] Supreme Court Justice Ruth Bader Ginsburg cited our *Deal* case for the proposition that we

---

17 Hamilton County perfected the role of "sore loser." After the Sixth Circuit Court of Appeals ruled against Hamilton County and denied its motion for reconsideration, the school system made one final appeal attempt before the U.S. Supreme Court. The high court rejected Hamilton County's appeal petition, which meant that the Sixth Circuit's ruling against Hamilton County would stand. The Sixth Circuit's ruling in *Deal* continues to this day and has been cited more than 250 times by other courts.

18 Hamilton County's lawyers included The Weatherly Firm, an Atlanta-based law firm known for representing school districts in high-profile cases.

19 In *Schaffer v. Weast,* a split Supreme Court ruled that in IDEA cases, the student bears the burden of proof on whether the school system offered the student a "free and appropriate public education." However, individual states are free to legislate otherwise. New York and New Jersey, for example, have adopted legislation placing that threshold burden on the school district.

cannot always rely on school systems to do the right thing. Justice Ginsburg wrote "Understandably, school districts striving to balance their budgets, if '[l]eft to [their] own devices,' will favor educational options that enable them to conserve resources.")[20]

After the *Deal* decision became final, word spread of the millions of dollars Hamilton County and its counsel had wasted. Around this time, more school districts began to accept Applied Behavior Analysis as an effective, if not "best practices" core teaching methodology.[21] The Surgeon General's report validating ABA's efficacy went a long way toward establishing that point. So did the multivolume set of findings and recommendations published by the New York State Department of Health. This time frame represented the turning point for Applied Behavior Analysis in our nation's public schools. Almost overnight, public school systems began to talk about the ostensible quality of *their* ABA programs and support personnel.[22]

For parents, the takeaway from the *Deal* case is that parents should be on the lookout for any situation where the school district has "predetermined" its program and placement recommendation. A parent's right to have meaningful participation at the IEP means much more than a parent's mere physical presence at the meeting. Any evidence of predetermination should be preserved. A school district may be entitled to reject a parent's request, but only after giving it due consideration. If the school district flat-out refuses to discuss a parental request, it probably is time to consult with counsel.

Making Plan B Work

Just as autism is considered a spectrum disorder, self-sufficiency and independence have their own continuums. While each student's potential for independence and self-sufficiency will vary widely, school-age programming that allows for learned helplessness in adulthood will translate to far greater public costs over an individual's lifetime. There is no way to accurately calculate these costs, but given the 50,000-plus Americans with

---

20 In 2016, in *T.K. v. NYCDOE*, the Second Circuit Court of Appeals cited the Deal precedent for the proposition that it is a violation of the federal IDEA statute when school districts impermissibly "predetermine" issues that are supposed to be fleshed out at the IEP meeting. The Hamilton County school system was back again in the news in 2018. In *L.H. v. Hamilton County Department of Education,* the Sixth Circuit reversed and remanded the district court's ruling in a decision that, to say the least, was highly critical the "least restrictive environment" arguments Hamilton County and its attorneys had advanced. No law firm wants to receive a court ruling noting that some of its arguments are "bizarre," disingenuous," or "without merit." See *L.H. v. Hamilton County Department of Education,* reversed and remanded (6th Cir. 8/20/18).

21 This is not to say that ABA works for every child, or that ABA alone will be sufficient. Many students on the spectrum will need additional interventions from the school system, including speech and language therapy, occupational therapy, physical therapy, and social skills training.

22 These early efforts by school districts often drew litigation fire, particularly when the school district relied on ineffective "group" teaching or instructors with little or no training or supervision.

autism who transition to adulthood each year, it is safe to say that billions of dollars are at stake annually. It is axiomatic that dollars and energy invested early to promote greater independence and self-sufficiency translate to significantly reduced public costs going forward. One thing is certain: the choices we make today will have far-reaching fiscal and social consequences for generations to come.

There is only so much time before the inevitable transition to adulthood. With the intervention clock ticking away, how should parents and school districts collaborate? How do they best "invest" their time and energy to make effective choices that will promote *sustainable* learning, independence, and self-sufficiency? Since school districts come to the table with far greater financial resources and leverage, what steps can parents take to level the playing field? As the generalization process is so critical to developing independence, how can parents promote generalization if the school district fails to do so in a meaningful way? Similarly, how can parents be proactive in encouraging the school district to timely provide appropriate "transition" related supports and programming? For implementing Plan B, what is the best way for parents to "land the plane?"

In these difficult and uncertain times, now more than ever, the autism community desperately needs a Declaration of Independence. In the chapters to come, I will explore the rights, entitlements, accommodations, and, perhaps most importantly, the practical strategies parents can employ to afford their children the opportunity to fulfill Congress' intent that they "lead productive and independent adult lives, to the *maximum extent possible*." In other words, fulfilling what every parent wants for their child.

Chapter 2
What Does the Right to a "Free Appropriate Public Education" Mean for My Child?

Looking back over the last 40 years, the demand for effective, individualized programming has been the spark igniting many unhelpful, wasteful lawsuits between parents and school districts in the pursuit of a FAPE (that is, the statutory right to a "free and appropriate public education").

Until relatively recently, most of the nation was focused on providing basic *access* to what the federal courts refer to as the "floor of educational opportunity" (see for example 1982's *Board of Education v. Rowley*, 458 U.S. 176, 201).[23] Advocacy groups applauded these early "access" decisions as landmark civil rights victories.

Providing access to the schoolhouse door and removing some of the barriers of exclusion certainly was a noble start, but it was not nearly enough. After watching the engine of the federal IDEA statute running rough for more than two decades, Congress realized that merely guaranteeing access to basic educational opportunities would not be sufficient to produce good outcomes. Today's IDEA statute, as amended, clearly explains its intent and purpose to meet the "unique needs" of children with autism and other disabilities and prepare them for "further education, employment, and independent living." Nevertheless, most federal court decisions through 2016 continued to be primarily access-oriented, recognizing only the "basic floor of opportunity."

Starting as far back as 1982 with the Supreme Court's access-oriented decision in *Board of Education of the Hendrick Hudson Central School District v. Rowley*, 458 U.S.176

---

23 I had the pleasure of meeting Clifford Rowley at a symposium sponsored by New York Law School. Mr. Rowley, the father of Amy Rowley (the student at issue in the *Rowley* case) reported that his daughter went on to earn a PhD and is now a university professor in California.

(1982),[24] courts have ruled, time and again, that making sure that special needs students reach their full potential is *not* a standard that school districts are obligated to meet. Even today, unlike the higher "best interests of the child" standard applicable in a family court matter, there is no requirement in an IDEA case for the court to do what is "best" for the student.

What, then, is the standard? Is mediocrity (or worse) really the school district's *objective*? A 2017 landmark decision from the United States Supreme Court has finally answered those fundamental questions, defining the contours of a new, markedly higher national standard with the potential to propel students who are on the spectrum to far greater levels of independence.

The Impact of the Supreme Court's 2017 Groundbreaking Decision in Endrew F.

It is relatively unusual for the entire U.S. Supreme Court to agree on anything. However, in March 2017, the high court unanimously mandated a new and more robust educational standard that went far beyond "access to the floor of educational opportunity."

In *Endrew F. v. Douglas County School District*, the Tenth Circuit Court of Appeals had ruled in a Colorado case that school districts only needed to provide an "educational benefit [that is] merely more than *de minimis*" (defined as too trivial or minor to merit consideration, especially in law). This standard is sometimes referred to as the "some benefit" standard. A unanimous Supreme Court reversed and rejected the "some benefit" standard as markedly inadequate, explaining:

---

[24] I have followed the Supreme Court since the days when I was a student at Georgetown. Georgetown's law school is located just blocks from the high court and I made it my business to observe many of the arguments after first stopping at the court cafeteria to grab a delicious, federally subsidized breakfast. At my table one rainy morning sat an unassuming man wearing ankle-high work boots and a plaid shirt. "You look very familiar," I said. "Really, how so?" said the man. I asked him a series of questions until finally, I asked "Just what do you do?" Smiling, the man said "Basically, I come to this building most days. After I have my usual breakfast, I go upstairs, put on a black robe and sit on a bench with a bunch of other people wearing the same outfit." The unassuming man sitting at my breakfast table that morning was then Chief Justice William Rehnquist. Three years later, in 1982, Chief Justice Rehnquist was to write the majority decision in *Rowley*, the first occasion for the high court to attempt to define the statutory entitlement to the "free and appropriate public education" (FAPE) mandated by the federal IDEA statute. One of Justice Rehnquist's law clerks from that period was John Roberts, currently the Chief Justice. How perfect that almost 35 years to the day after the *Rowley* decision, Chief Justice Roberts would write for a unanimous, 8-0 Court in *Endrew F.*, clarifying the meaning and scope of the statutory FAPE standard.

1. [FAPE is] "markedly **more demanding** than the merely more than de minimis test."
2. The student's IEP is "the centerpiece of the statute's education delivery system for disabled children."
3. [FAPE is an education] "reasonably calculated to enable a child to make progress appropriate in light of the child's circumstances."
4. "For a student who is not fully integrated in the regular classroom and not able to achieve on grade level the educational program must be **appropriately ambitious** in light of his circumstances."
5. "The goals may differ but every child should have the chance to meet **challenging objectives.**"
6. "An IEP is not a form document. It is constructed only after careful consideration of the child's present levels of achievement, disability and **potential** for growth."

The high court's unanimous decision in *Endrew F.*[25] represents an unmistakable message to the nation's school districts: When the district develops and offers the student an Individualized Educational Plan, it must be appropriately challenging and ambitious in relation to the student's potential, unique needs, and circumstances. It is no longer defensible for school systems to aim for the mere "floor" of educational access. The "some benefit" standard is no more. Because of the decision in *Endrew F.*, school districts are now required to aim for a higher trajectory—one likely to result in significantly better outcomes for sustainable learning and greater levels of independence and self-sufficiency. Good news for the autism community.

---

25 My law firm served as *amicus* counsel to Autism Speaks in *Endrew F.*

Chapter 3
Generalization: The Critical "Missing Link" to Promote Independence and Self-Sufficiency

Autism is a highly nuanced, multifaceted "spectrum" disorder. Just as no two individuals have the same fingerprints, no two individuals with autism present with identical features. The Diagnostic and Statistical Manual, Fifth Edition (DSM-V) provides the currently recognized diagnostic criteria for Autism Spectrum Disorder. These same criteria are key factors that collectively interfere and "compete" with the process of developing greater levels of independence and self-sufficiency:

- ✓ "Persistent deficits in social communication and social interaction across multiple contexts...as manifested by deficits in social emotional reciprocity...deficits in nonverbal communicative behaviors used for social interaction...deficits in developing, maintaining and understanding relationships"
- ✓ "Restricted, repetitive patterns of behavior, interests, or activities"
- ✓ "Stereotyped or repetitive motor movements, use of objects, or speech"
- ✓ "Insistence on sameness, inflexible adherence to routines, or ritualized patterns of verbal or nonverbal behavior"
- ✓ "Highly restricted, fixated interests that are abnormal in intensity or focus"
- ✓ "Hyper or hyperactivity to sensory input or unusual interest in sensory aspects of the environment"[26]

---

[26] A somewhat controversial change in the fifth edition of the Diagnostic and Statistical Manual provides that "Individuals with a well-established DSM-IV diagnosis of autistic disorder, Asperger's disorder, or pervasive developmental disorder not otherwise specified should be given the diagnosis of autism spectrum disorder [ASD]." In the prior (fourth) edition of the DSM, Asperger's had been categorized as a diagnosis separate and apart from autism spectrum disorder.

We cannot afford to lose sight of the fact that so many children with autism have difficulty "generalizing" their skills. However, generalization is something that can be taught—and must be taught, given that it's the key to sustainable learning. As such, teaching and promoting the process of generalization is absolutely critical to developing greater levels of independence and self-sufficiency.

While most neurotypical children are born with the capacity to learn incidentally by observing the behaviors of others, there is consensus in the field that many, if not most, students with autism have great difficulty learning in that way. When a student with autism is painstakingly taught a skill "in isolation," that same student often will then have great difficulty "generalizing" that skill across different environmental settings or with different individuals. Professor Shirley Cohen, cofounder of New York City's ASD NEST Program, writes about this phenomenon in her book, *Targeting Autism:* "Autistic children don't learn much in the natural course of childhood activities and do not generalize from one situation to another *unless their instructional programs give them extensive practice in doing so.*"[27]

Just to learn the color red, a student with autism may need to be presented with that color in all its hues and manifestations (e.g. a red ball, ketchup, a red ribbon, a red car, etc.). Over time, with practice, the student eventually learns to generalize what "red" is. Then you'd need to apply that time-consuming, painstaking, brick-by-brick process to all of the remaining colors and the many other things a child needs to learn to function in this world. This process also includes learning to generalize skills in the context of behavior and social communication.

While clinicians in the field agree strongly that the generalization process is critical for students with autism becoming more independent, virtually all pre-*Andrew F.* federal court decisions steadfastly followed the proposition that teaching to generalization is *beyond* what school districts are obligated to provide (see *River City School Board, Thompson R2-J School District v. Luke P.*). This errant approach is akin to knowing that a plane must fly faster than 767 miles per hour to break the sound barrier, yet implementing an arbitrary policy that planes shall not fly any faster than 700 miles per hour (i.e. fast, but not fast *enough* to break through the barrier).

---

[27] I met Professor Cohen more than 20 years ago at an autism conference sponsored by Mt. Sinai Hospital's Seaver Center. With the midday break nearing, I invited Professor Cohen to have lunch with me at the iconic, now closed, Carnegie Delicatessen. After we had thoroughly gorged ourselves on potato pancakes and overstuffed corned beef and pastrami sandwiches, I was embarrassed to discover that I had left my wallet at home, proving once again that (at least for Professor Cohen), there is no such thing as a free lunch.

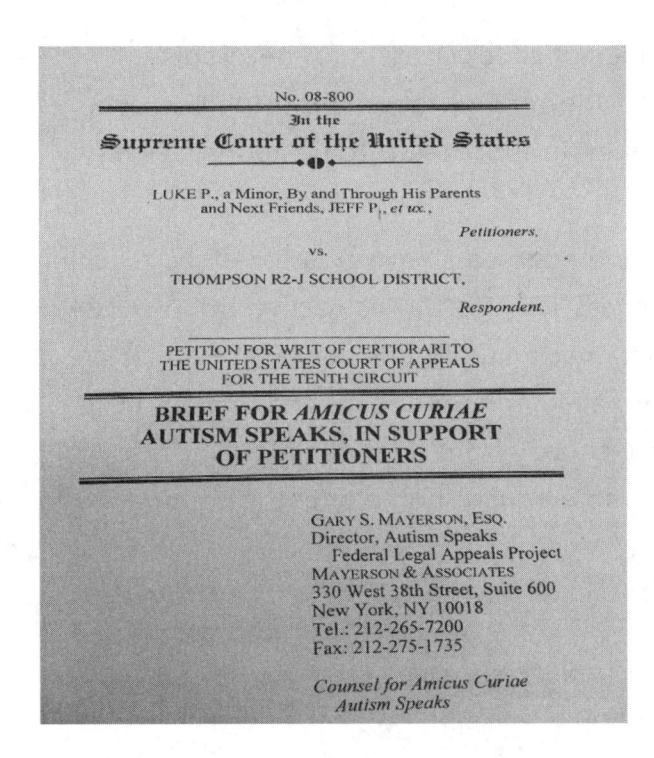

In the *Luke P.* case, then-judge Neil Gorsuch held that promoting generalization is not necessary to ensure a compliant IEP, reversing two administrative decisions and the decision of the federal district court. Judge Gorsuch based his finding upon the "merely more than *di minimis*" FAPE standard being followed by the Tenth Circuit—the very "some benefit" standard that the Supreme Court later rejected as "markedly" inadequate in the *Endrew F.* case.

In *Luke P.*, I submitted an *amicus* brief on behalf of Autism Speaks in support of the student's petition to appeal Judge Gorsuch's decision to the Supreme Court, arguing that the Tenth Circuit's bare-bones "some benefit" educational standard was too low to be "reasonably calculated." The high court unanimously embraced that argument years later in the *Endrew F.* case, but it unfortunately was not ready to make that leap back in 2008. What a difference a decade makes![28]

The federal IDEA statute does not and cannot guarantee a student's outcome. However, as clarified by the Supreme Court in *Endrew F.*, it does guarantee an education that is "reasonably calculated to enable a child to make progress appropriate in light of the child's circumstances." It also mandates an "appropriately ambitious" and "challenging" educational program developed collaboratively after "careful consideration" of the child's potential and other relevant circumstances.

If a student allegedly "learns" a skill but never generalizes and *sustains* that skill, what has the student actually learned? A student's IEP is required to be "reasonably calculated" to make meaningful progress. For many students with autism, a strong argument can be made that teaching programs that do not meaningfully promote skill generalization does not meet FAPE's "reasonably calculated" standard. Parents, however, should not wait for the federal court system to come around. Nor should they wait for assistance from school districts that will be under increasing fiscal pressures

---

28 Better late than never, understand that when we are talking about the Supreme Court's decision-making, the process is almost always evolutionary, not revolutionary.

for the foreseeable future. Given the importance of generalization for developing independence, parents need to constantly provide generalization opportunities, even if the school district does not. Teaching for generalization needs to be added to every teaching program and protocol.

After decades of trial and error, clinicians and educators have greatly refined teaching methods that promote the generalization process. Dr. Amy Davies-Lackey, BCBA-D, LBA, the Director of Education for the renowned Manhattan Childrens Center in Manhattan, explains in Appendix A , Generalization Toward a More Independent and Enriched Life (page 169) how teaching to generalization differs today from prior decades. She also identifies some approaches that parents can implement at home or in the community to promote the generalization process.

Chapter 4
Managing Your Child's Right to Be Educated in the "Least Restrictive Environment"

If you are the parent of a child on the autism spectrum, you celebrate every achievement. You will commemorate many milestones that most other parents will take for granted. Arguably, the greatest challenge for children on the spectrum is learning how to make and sustain friendships: It's a big day when your child is invited to a playdate. It can also really sting to learn that every child in your child's classroom (except yours) was invited to a birthday party. Perhaps one day in the not-too-distant future, we might see a bumper sticker proclaiming, "I am the proud parent of a student with autism who made a friend at school."

One Mother's Story

The following personal story might illustrate this best:

> Consider the following synonyms for "inclusion": admittance, formation, incorporation, involvement, composition, embodiment, embracement, encompassment.
>
> Many years ago, it was a weekday. It was a brisk, clear blue, early spring day. I was outside running laps at the local high-school track. As I was leaving, I saw a class of young children, kindergarteners or first-graders, in a line, a common **formation** entering the track field. All the children were paired up, each pair was holding hands. The gym teacher was at the head of the line, holding hands with one of the students—it was clear to me that this was a student with autism. Intuitively, parents "in the know" immediately spot this.
>
> I watched the line of children, this **composition**, proceed forward. I was glad to see that the child with autism was holding hands with the gym teacher. I also

was glad to see that the child with autism was at the head of the line. I thought that not too long ago, in my school district, this child would have been at the very end of the line, holding hands with an aide, if the child was lucky. And then, not too long before that, this student would have been in a separate class with only special education students. Or a separate school. I thought, so this is what progress looks like.

I considered the years, the sweat, parental angst, and advocacy it took to get here—to have this student be recognized and to have "earned the right" to be at the front of the line. How much education, training, and resources had been allocated to the school staff and the community for this simple act to occur?

I thought about the implications of having this child holding the gym teacher's hand and standing first in line. What exactly did this show the rest of the class? How did this "look" to the student's peers? What did this "say" about the student's needs? It was highly doubtful that the gym teacher held a different student's hand in each class—or even held a student's hand at all.

I then thought about the likelihood that this could stigmatize the student—that this well-intentioned act of visible "inclusion" could actually have the opposite effect. Perhaps this was a display that could easily be implemented—one that might appease us and make us feel good about ourselves at the expense of the child's needs, potential social opportunities, and self-image.

I went from glad to sad as I watched the student at the head of the line appear to disconnect, to somehow separate from his peers, perhaps facilitated by this simple act of inclusion, this **embracement**. My instincts proved correct. I watched as the students spread out and played together on the field, while the student who just moments before stood first in line now stood off to the side, alone with an aide.

Truly, the most appropriate **embodiment** and the most appropriate **inclusion** would be to allow the child to be **incorporated**—to be inside the line, to be in line *with* peers.

I hope for the day when the student with autism stands in the middle of the line, holding hands with a peer. Now *that* would be progress. That would be **involvement**, which is where we have to go.

Parents will continue to have angst and to advocate and to educate. Step-by-step, parents lead us all forward, so that our children with special needs may be included in the middle, where they rightly belong, **embraced** on both sides.

And one day, even the parents "in the know" will not be able to discern a child's exclusion.

What is the "Least Restrictive Environment?

The statutory mandate to educate students in their "least restrictive environment" represents a critical factor for developing greater levels of independence and self-sufficiency. The applicable statutory mandate offers a continuum that requires that children with disabilities be educated with their non-disabled peers to the "maximum extent appropriate"—*even if* implementing the mandate means that the student must be provided with additional supports to be successful. Section 1412(a)(5)(A) of the federal Individuals with Disabilities Education Act expressly requires that:

> "To the **maximum extent appropriate,** children with disabilities ... [must be] educated with children who are not disabled, and ... special classes, separate schooling, or other removal of children with disabilities from the regular education environment [shall] occur only when the nature or severity of the disability is such that education in regular classes with the use of supplementary aids and services cannot be achieved satisfactorily."

The public health and safety concerns regarding maintaining safe social distances will likely now be factored in by the court system as a component of the statutory mandate. Congress, without knowing it at the time, crafted the statute to allow for such a contingency by using the qualifier "appropriate." Safety and health are always number one. Accordingly, I anticipate that smaller class sizes are in the offing so long as virus spread remains a concern.

Some school districts will argue that if your child needs extra supports and services to be successful in a mainstream classroom, he or she should probably be educated in a self-contained classroom. This kind of argument flies smack in the face of the statutory protections. It is essential for parents to know that students are not required to "earn" the right to be educated in their least restrictive environment: Congress favors the less restrictive setting even if it requires a one-to-one aide or other accommodations. Who would ever exclude someone from the pleasure of reading a book just because they might need the support of eyeglasses to do so? Could you imagine anyone forbidding a person from walking because they need the support of a cane or crutches?

Similarly, Congress has mandated that students be considered for educational inclusion *even if* doing so will require a one-to-one aide and other support services and *even if* the student might theoretically learn more in a more restrictive setting—unless the student cannot learn "satisfactorily" with support in the less restrictive setting. See, for example, *L.B. v. Nebo School District*, 379 F.3d 966 (10th Cir. 2004); *Zachary Deal v. Hamilton County Department of Education*, 392 F.3d 840 (6th Cir. 2004);[29] and *L.H. v. Hamilton County Department of Education*, No. 18-5086 (6th Cir. 2018) rejecting school district's unduly restrictive approach.

Mainstream and inclusionary settings can offer unique "modeling" and other related benefits that may not be available in more restrictive settings. According to Dr. David Salsberg,[30] a well-known pediatric neuropsychologist based in Manhattan: "Even with significant support provided in and out of the classroom, not every student with autism will be able to meaningfully benefit from a mainstream or other inclusion experience. However, those who are able to do so will have the benefit of excellent models for behavior, communication, and socialization."[31]

However, the statutory entitlement to be educated in the least restrictive environment comes with a weighty caveat: The ability of the *other* students in the classroom to learn with the inclusion of the special needs student also must be considered. Accordingly, if a student—despite the support of a behavior plan, a Board Certified Behavior Analyst, and one-to-one support in the classroom—is constantly aggressive toward other students or engaging in disruptive behavior preventing the other children in the classroom from learning, a more structured and restrictive setting will need to be considered for that student.

Accordingly, a student's statutory right to be educated in the least restrictive environment is not absolute—it can sometimes involve a thoughtful balancing and reconciling of competing interests. The problem is that too many school districts fail to engage in the requisite analysis and will "default" to an unduly restrictive placement at the first sign of difficulty. This knee-jerk response is what Congress intended to avoid. The presumption should be that the student be educated in the *less* restrictive setting.

The importance of public perception and attitudes toward inclusion cannot be overstated. In 2004, the well known and progressive cartoonist Ted Rall ignited a

---

29 In *Deal*, the first autism case to reach the U.S. Supreme Court, the Court rejected the school system's appeal petition. The high court left undisturbed the Sixth Circuit's core "inclusion" finding that, procedurally, the school district's failures at the student's IEP meeting precluded any meaningful discussion about satisfying Congress' "least restrictive environment" mandate.

30 Dr. Salsberg contributed Appendix B (page 175), concerning the factors he looks for when observing or otherwise looking at a school placement to ascertain whether its resources meet a student's needs.

31 It is possible to find poor models in a mainstream classroom—or good models in a self-contained classroom. There are always exceptions. In general, however, the behavioral, communication, and socialization profiles of students in less restrictive classroom settings show more effectiveness than those of students in more restrictive settings.

firestorm of controversy and criticism with an offensive and hurtful cartoon that reinforced highly negative stereotypes about inclusion and its presumed adverse impact on the "other" students. Despite Rall's profuse and heartfelt apologies, the *Washington Post* promptly dropped Rall in response.

More than a decade later, just prior to the 2016 presidential election, then-candidate Donald Trump was criticized for mocking a *New York Times* reporter with a disability. Trump flatly denied having done so and many took the position that he had done nothing wrong.

We can enact the laws and conventions (and use other legal instruments) to establish policy and recognize a legal *right* to inclusive education. Having the legal *right* to inclusion, however, does not ensure acceptance and effective implementation, particularly if the school district, teaching staff, or parent body are resistant to inclusion. School administrators and teachers set the tone for whether or not the "welcome mat" will be put out in a real sense. If a school principal is perceived by school staff as being "anti-inclusion," there is a tendency for other school personnel to follow suit.[32]

Just as autism is considered a "spectrum" disorder, inclusion comes with its own spectrum and continuum.[33] Inclusion programs, therefore, need to be shaped to meet the unique needs of the student. In addition, while many children with autism can meaningfully benefit from educational inclusion with appropriate supports and accommodations, we continue to see situations where physical inclusion with neurotypical students is being invoked as a pretextual excuse to justify the school system's failure to provide adequate special education services.

---

32 In *The Wizard of Oz*, Glinda asks Dorothy "Are you a good witch or a bad witch?" There are many special education administrators who are highly skilled and demonstrably care about the students and families that they serve. Unfortunately, some special education administrators will follow an ignoble agenda that requires intervention.

33 For instance, an inclusion experience may involve "reverse inclusion": injecting receptive and motivated neurotypical students into a self-contained classroom. Or, it might involve an integrated, co-teaching classroom taught by a special education teacher and a regular teacher. Or, the student with a disability may be included in a fully "mainstream" classroom designed for neurotypical students with supports, curriculum modifications, and accommodations. Or, it might include extracurricular activities, such as participation in team sports.

I was invited to speak at the United Nations on World Autism Awareness Day to discuss how developing nations without abundant financial resources can design and offer inclusion programs. At the conclusion of my presentation, the event moderator asked a pointed question that likely was on the minds of many: "Is inclusion for everyone?" I responded that there are far too many children with autism who are not being educated in inclusive settings, but are entitled to the benefits that inclusion would offer. I cautioned, however, that inclusion is not for everyone and should never be used to excuse a school district's failure to provide a special-needs student with special education support. At the end of the day, inclusion must mean a great deal more than a student simply breathing the same air as the other students in the classroom.

I have litigated cases involving Congress' "least restrictive environment" mandate in a variety of jurisdictions across the country including: Utah student *L.B. and K.B. v. Nebo School District*, 379 F.3d 966 (10th Cir. 2004); New Jersey student *D.L. and K.L. o/b/o J.L. v. Springfield Board of Education*, 2008 U.S. Dist. LEXIS 17727 (D. N.J. 2008); New York student *N.G. v. Kiryas Joel Free School District*, 777 F. Supp. 2d 606 (S.D.N.Y. 2011); and upstate New York student *T.M v. Cornwall Central School District*, 752 F.3d 145 (2d Cir. 2015).

The above court decisions are highly instructive in defining the scope Congress' "least restrictive environment" mandate. These cases demonstrate that (1) the least restrictive environment mandate starts immediately and extends to preschool situations; (2) the mandate can apply year-round and does *not* get to take a summer vacation; (3) parents do not have to first "try out" a more restrictive setting to have the right to file for a hearing; (4) "least restrictive" actually means the least restrictive, not just less restrictive; and (5) the mandate presupposes that a student may require additional supports to be successful in the less restrictive setting—i.e., students do not have to earn the right to be educated and supported in their least restrictive environment.

The least restrictive environment can be a double-edged sword. Sometimes, it's the parent challenging a school district's program as unduly restrictive. Or the school district may invoke the concept to attack parents who have implemented programming in the home, or those who send their children to residential programs where the school district genuinely believes that the child can be satisfactorily educated in a "day school" setting.

How, then, do parents know if and when their child is ready to meaningfully benefit from an inclusion experience? They might turn to an educational consultant with specific inclusion training and experience—preferably someone without financial interest in the student's ongoing program. That consultant can assess a child to ascertain if enough prerequisite skills have been mastered to be in that kind of a setting and the related question of which aids and supports might also be needed (e.g. modifications to the general curriculum, proximate seating, a classroom aide and/or resource room support, extra time during tests, note-taking support, etc.)

Appendix B (page 175), contributed by noted pediatric neuropsychologist David Salsberg, provides a useful overview of what he looks for when assessing the qualities, resources, and conditions of a school setting under consideration for a student. Parents observing and assessing school options may want to consider the same kinds of factors.

As explained in Chapter 5 (page 51), there is a statutory mechanism that, if applicable, can help parents obtain, at the school district's expense, an independent evaluation of a student's functioning in the inclusion setting. Ultimately, even in a situation where a student is considered an excellent candidate for inclusion, there must be a good match with an appropriate school. Even then, some adjustments will still probably be needed.[34]

For example, if classroom aide support is considered necessary, will the aide be perceived by the student and his peers as someone who is assigned and attached to the student, or will the aide's role be disguised as a "classroom" aide in the interest of creating a more natural setting? Similarly, if the student's IEP contains mandates for speech therapy or other related services, will those services be delivered on a "push in" (in the classroom) basis, or will the student need to be "pulled out" to access those services? If data will be taken, who is responsible for taking and analyzing that data? What should the parents be working on at home to reinforce what is going on at school? And at the end of the day, how will progress in the inclusion setting be measured?

---

[34] Parents and school districts should not expect an inclusion site to be effective "as-is." If an inclusion site is going to work, parents and school districts need to be ready, willing, and able to make adjustments as needed.

Chapter 5
How Parents Can Obtain Independent Evaluations at School District Expense

Choosing the right assessments early can be critical to ascertaining a student's unique profile of strengths and challenges and making the appropriate recommendations to address those challenges. It is much harder for a school district to reject or dismiss a request when it has been recommended by a respected professional. Hearing officers and judges also tend to respect the opinions and recommendations of professionals. Accordingly, in situations where the IEP is in dispute, the resolution of that dispute can often turn on what some respected professional has recommended.

Today, with more and more assessments and IEP meetings being conducted remotely, there is a greater chance that disagreements will arise over assessment reliability. Parents may want to secure a "second opinion."

But what if the family can't afford a battery of private assessments? Is it sufficient for parents to rely upon the assessments conducted by the school district? It depends. Unfortunately, far too many school districts will accept (or request) evaluations that do *not* conclude with specific recommendations. According to the school districts that follow this all-too-common practice, the purpose of this limitation is not to save the school district money, but to free the IEP team to make up its own mind. But what IEP team would not want a professional's recommendation before making those decisions? If school district administrators are concerned that a professional's opinion might pressure school personnel regarding a student's IEP, this actually speaks to the persuasive power of such professional recommendations.

Paying an experienced evaluator good money to "hold back" from expressing a professional opinion on the services the student requires is a halfhearted approach that makes absolutely no sense. Any quality evaluation should make specific recommendations designed to meet the student's unique needs after carefully teasing out the student's strengths and challenges. If the IEP team has a problem with those recommendations, they have every right to say so (subject of course to being overruled by a judge or hearing officer).

Private evaluators who don't answer to school district administrators don't have any incentive to hold back. For this reason, parents with the financial resources often secure private evaluations to speed up the IEP development process. This approach can be very helpful for families who can take on these expenses, but parents should bear in mind that these private evaluations do not impact the school district's right to request conducting its own assessments of the student. If the school district requests its own assessments, parents should normally consent; a refusal can result in serious adverse consequences later on.

So what should parents do if they disagree with the school district's evaluations? What if, for example, the school district's evaluations conclude that the student should be in a self-contained classroom and the parents are absolutely convinced that their child would benefit from a less restrictive setting? Worse still, what should parents do if the school district was supposed to evaluate the student, but failed to do so? How can a parent with modest or no financial resources gain access to quality private evaluations that can lead to quality programming and improved outcomes?

The answer lies in an important procedural right outlined in the IDEA statute: the parent's statutory right to an *independent* evaluation at school district expense. This is an important entitlement that can help level the playing field, especially for families with limited financial resources. The entitlement, however, comes with a few conditions and limitations.

Pursuant to 34 C.F.R. [Code of Federal Regulations] Sec. 300.502, *if a parent disagrees with an evaluation obtained by the school district, the parent has the right to obtain an independent educational evaluation at no cost.*[35] This right refers to an evaluation that is administered by someone who is truly independent and not employed by the school district. For this reason, parents are not required to choose evaluators from the school district's "list" maintained for that purpose. Nor are parents automatically required to accept the school district's pre-set limits on the amount it will pay for an independent evaluation. Parents should not be required to pay anything out of pocket for the independent evaluation.

---

35 If a hearing officer requests an independent evaluation during the course of a hearing, that too is at no cost to the parent.

The school district has 30 days to take action once a parental request for an independent evaluation is made. The school district may ask a parent to give a reason for the objection to the school district's evaluation. However, if the school district denies the parent's request, the burden then falls *on the school district* to file for a hearing where the assigned hearing officer will either agree with the school district's position or order it to pay for the independent evaluation that the parent had requested.

A due process hearing is time-consuming and expensive. The school district's mounting costs in proceeding to a hearing for even one day (hiring counsel, paying the hearing officer and the court reporter, paying and arranging for substitute teachers, etc.) would likely exceed the cost of the requested independent evaluation. For that reason, unless there are extraordinary circumstances, most school districts will simply opt to pay for an independent evaluation at a parent's request. In all circumstances, the school district is required to *consider* any independent evaluation, regardless of who pays for it.

What happens if the school district refuses the parent's request for an independent evaluation without filing for a hearing, as the statute requires? In that scenario, the parent can and should file for a hearing. If the parent prevails with the assistance of counsel, the parent can make an application for attorneys' fees in addition to any reimbursement relief ordered by the hearing officer.

When parents request funding for an independent evaluation, it is imperative to document the request. Letters are fine. Faxes are fine. Emailed requests also are entirely acceptable. Under no circumstances, however, should parents rely upon an oral request. Oral requests are often ignored and all too easy to forget. It is critical to make an appropriate record.

Requests for independent evaluations look something like the following:

Dr. Peter Stone
Committee on Special Education
Shady Lane School District

Re: Alex Singleton D.O.B. 11/14/2015

Dear Dr. Stone:

Respectfully, we are dissatisfied with the speech evaluation administered by Sherry Walcott. Ms. Walcott spent only 15 minutes assessing Alex and did not address many of the problems we are seeing. In all candor, the report we received from Ms. Walcott seems sparse and unduly generic.

In light of the above, we are requesting approval and funding to secure an independent evaluation from Dr. Brenda Witt. Dr. Witt charges $2500 for a comprehensive speech and language evaluation and we will, of course, timely share the results with your office. Thank you for your consideration. Please advise ASAP whether the district will fund the requested independent evaluation, as Dr. Witt's appointment calendar fills up quickly.

Sincerely,
Bob and Joan Singleton

NOTE: *Parents should share the results of the independent evaluation with the IEP team. If the independent evaluation recommends additional or different services or programming that the school district is not providing, the parent should request that the IEP team convene to consider those recommendations. By statute, the school district is required to do so.*

Chapter 6
How Parents Can Manage and Shape the IEP Process

The Individualized Educational Plan (IEP) is recognized by the federal court system as being the "centerpiece" of every eligible student's special education program. Broadly speaking, the IEP is intended to reflect the student's unique needs and the school district's plan to address those needs. In many respects, the IEP functions as a form of contract or "bill of rights" between the student/parents and the school district.[36]

The recent pandemic-caused school closures delayed, but did not stop the IEP development process. Many if not most school districts learned to conduct IEP meetings by telephone, Zoom, or other communication technology. Parents and administrators adapted so that the IEP process could continue. Even after the nation's schools reopen, we can expect to see school districts asking parents to consent to IEP meetings being conducted remotely. That decision will have to be made on a case-by-case basis.

When immersed in the IEP development process and its special language, it's important not to lose sight of the fact that beneath all the evaluations, assessments, and progress reports, there exists a living, breathing child with highly unique needs.

Be Aware of Sequence Changes and Evidence of Predetermination

Discussions at the IEP meeting are supposed to follow a certain *sequence*. Roughly, the recognized sequence of issues entails: an assessment of the student's present levels of performance; eligibility for special education services; classification (e.g. autism, learning disabled, etc.); the development of goals and objectives; the timing, duration, and location of services, behavioral support, school placement, accommodations, and modifications; eligibility for ESY (extended school year) programming; participation in

---

[36] The end of this chapter explores the salient differences between an IEP and a Section 504 Plan.

standard assessments; "transition" planning (for students whose age triggers transition support); transportation support; and how, if at all, the student will be included in general education classes.

Not all school districts will follow the recognized sequence; some will leapfrog over the foundational components of the IEP meeting to save time or because it has already *predetermined* the student's placement and program. If you are a parent and this happens at your IEP meeting, do not lecture your school district about its failure to follow the required sequence—just make a note to yourself on what sequence the school district actually followed.

The IEP is supposed to be developed collaboratively, with the student's parents (and sometimes the student) as full-fledged members of the IEP team, following the receipt of notice and an invitation to attend. Many conflicts arise in the situation where the school district fails to accord parents this basic protocol. This is not to say that parents have the right to dictate to the school district. However, a school district that fails to meaningfully include the student's parents as equal members of the IEP team will do so at its peril.

The IEP meeting notice date is not written in stone. If the meeting date is not convenient for parents, they are entitled to request an adjournment, proposing other dates that would work. If you are a parent facing this situation, make sure to communicate the adjournment request in writing (email is fine).

There exists a "good faith obligation" for parents and school districts to share reports and other important information.[37] The idea is that the IEP team should be informed by the available reports and information before it makes any decisions about a student's future. The failure to share reports and important information in a timely manner can have serious consequences down the line. If you are having any thoughts of not sharing a report, you probably need to have a discussion with counsel.

The IEP team might include the required functionaries (i.e. the parent, special education teacher, regular education teacher, school psychologist, and the school district's designated representative). In other instances, the school district might choose to send *dozens* of attendees. Parents also have the right to invite and bring attendees of

---

[37] For example, if a student under the care of a physician begins to take a medication for distractibility, this information should be shared with the school district. The same would be true if a student should cease taking medication. The same would also be true if the school district came into possession of a progress report from the student's teacher noting and admitting the student's lack of progress. There is little upside for withholding important information that should be shared as part of the "collaborative" approach that Congress and the Supreme Court expects.

their choosing to the meeting.[38]

The Supreme Court's landmark 2017 decision in the *Endrew F.* case guarantees that whether you live in New York or in New Mexico, your child is entitled to a "challenging" and "ambitious" IEP that takes his or her unique needs and potential into account. To meet this new national standard, your child's IEP must now be "reasonably calculated" to promote *meaningful* educational progress. No longer will "merely more than *de minimus*" (the "some benefit" test) be considered an acceptable FAPE standard. The new standard is "markedly" higher.

Preserve Any Evidence of Intimidation Tactics

Let me be the first to say that the overwhelming majority of school district administrators are informed, caring, and compassionate human beings who genuinely are ready, willing, and able to do the right thing. If an honest mistake is made, they will promptly rectify it. These are the kind of administrators you want in your corner.

Unfortunately, the reason my phone rings as often as it does is because some school district administrators are overwhelmed or are following entirely different agendas or mandates that have little, if anything, to do with addressing or meeting the child's unique needs. In the latter scenario, it is important for parents to be sensitive to the kinds of things some school district administrators will say at IEP meetings in an effort to intimidate parents to give their consent for implementing the school district's proposed IEP.[39] The following examples are illustrative:

- ✓ "This is public school. Do you know how much this school district spends on special education programs? What you are asking for is just not in the budget. Perhaps you should look into a private school."
- ✓ "As a loving parent, we know you want what is *best* for your child, but we are not required to provide an optimal program."
- ✓ "We want to get services started for your child right away, but we cannot do so until you give your consent to the IEP."
- ✓ "I have been in this field for thirty years. Believe me, I know what I'm doing."

---

38 If a parent intends to bring counsel to the IEP meeting, this is something that should be disclosed in *advance* to the school district. Otherwise, the parents and their counsel may arrive for the IEP meeting only to see the meeting canceled and rescheduled to afford the school district the opportunity to have its counsel present.

39 If parents do not challenge the written IEP generated by the school district within 14 days, the school district is permitted to *implement* the IEP even in the absence of written consent. The flipside of any presumption of consent (based upon a failure to challenge the IEP within two weeks of receipt) is that parents can withdraw their consent at any time.

- ✓ "I would love to help you, but if I did, I'd be fired."
- ✓ "What you are asking for is a specific methodology. We are not permitted to discuss methodology."
- ✓ "You are fortunate to live in such a beautiful area. In this community, parents are expected to pay for their child's afterschool services. This is always a parent's 'choice.'"
- ✓ "If we were to give your child what you are requesting, it sets a precedent that would open the floodgates for other families to ask for the same thing. If we can't give it to everyone, we can't give it to only your child."
- ✓ "Why don't we at least start with something and see how it goes?"
- ✓ "We have had many families in your exact situation. Yours is the only family to have ever complained."
- ✓ "You really need to relax and leave things to the professionals."
- ✓ "The afterschool services you're seeking are excessive and would be harmful to your child. Your child needs 'downtime' just like all the other kids."
- ✓ "It's insulting and offensive that you ask so many challenging questions. Don't you trust us?"
- ✓ "Your family is going to be living in this school district for many years. Do you really want to start our relationship off on the wrong foot by being so demanding?"

Should Parents Ever Record Their IEP Meetings?

Parents should take good notes at the IEP meeting and be mindful to accurately record any questionable statements like the above examples. In general, though, unless the parties are already in serious conflict, I normally recommend *against* recording IEP meetings. There are few things less welcome than the moment a parent breaks out a recording device. The presence of a recording device at the IEP table can signal distrust and prevent the free-flowing dialogue that can be helpful to the IEP process. Even if there is justification in an unusual case to record the IEP meeting, no one should ever make a *surreptitious* recording of the IEP meeting. Not even if the IEP meeting is a phone conference where no one would ever know. It's simply wrong and hearing officers do not look kindly on conduct that has the appearance of a "setup."

Some Sources of Conflict at IEP Meetings

Why is there is so much conflict at IEP meetings involving students on the autism spectrum? One obvious source of conflict is the pervasive, 24/7 scope of the student's needs versus the limited, compressed schedule of the school day and calendar. Autism is a pervasive developmental disorder—a "workaholic" that does not know when it's time to take a break, holiday, or vacation.

Another possible culprit is the annual process of approving the school budget—a process that often comes with an *apologia* to the district's taxpayers who may ask pointedly why so much of the school budget is earmarked for special education "mandates." Some school district administrators are hired with a mandate to cut costs. School board members may fear the political fallout from higher property taxes. They, in turn, put pressure on the school district's superintendent. When special education administrators are brought in under those circumstances (whether those responsible will admit it or not), there is constant pressure to balance the school district's budget on the backs of the most vulnerable among us.

My Hungarian grandmother Charlotte understood these dynamics on a personal level. One of her favorite sayings was "When the wolf is at the door, love goes out the window."[40] When the school district's administrator becomes an endangered species for having overspent the special education budget, that administrator has a conflict and personal agenda that may interfere with parents who are on a mission to secure an appropriate and effective program.

Another main cause of conflict at IEP meetings is the level of training and expertise that is available "in-district." It is only natural that, whether it is true or not, special education personnel want to *believe* that they have all the training and expertise they need to do their jobs for any student who might come their way.

Few, if any, teachers will acknowledge to administrators that their skills and training are not up to the task at hand. There is an old saying that "in the land of the blind, the one-eyed man is king." Partially trained teachers might be able to get administrators to believe that they are autism experts simply by virtue of having more autism training than their supervisors. Partially informed administrators will then put the squeeze on parents to believe the same thing. There is a big difference, however, between virtual reality and, well, reality. Sometimes, ferreting out the truth requires hiring an educational consultant who knows the difference—and also knows how to explain that difference to third parties.

---

40 My Grandmother Charlotte was paralyzed from the waist down following risky spinal surgery. She got around pretty good using a walker. As a child, I once saw her mow her entire lawn in the hot Miami sun, gripping her walker with one hand and a manual lawnmower with the other. It took her hours, but she got the job done. Grandma Charlotte was one tough cookie. She focused her energy on what she was able to do rather than any obvious limitations.

Should Parents Ever Send Their Child to School with a Concealed Recording Device?

Once you entrust your child to the public-school system and they walk through the schoolhouse door, you are trusting that system to provide timely, accurate information on what your child is doing behind that door. What if parents are concerned that their child is exposed to some danger at school that's not being communicated? Can a parent ever send their child to school with a concealed recording device hidden in their clothing or backpack?

I am not a proponent of concealing recording equipment on a child (except perhaps in the extraordinary situation where the child is being abused or is in imminent danger of being harmed). A parent's mere curiosity is not sufficient. If, however, your child's safety is of genuine concern, according to the New York Court of Appeals, the answer in a state like New York is a qualified "maybe." Parents should be aware that in other states, surreptitious recording is a *crime*, so the answer would be an unequivocal "no." You don't want to face criminal charges for trying to protect your child. If you are even thinking of sending your child to school with a surreptitious recording device, no matter what state you live in, this is definitely something that warrants a discussion with your attorney.

Parents Should Normally Consent to School District Assessment Requests

Often, the school district will want to conduct its own assessments. The school district may present consent forms that need to be executed before any such (district-requested) assessments can take place. Parents do *not* have the right to refuse consent for school district-requested evaluations on the grounds that the parent "already" has secured (or is in the process of securing) private evaluations. Unless your counsel instructs you not to consent in a specific case, you should *always* give consent. Refusal to do so might later be construed by a hearing officer to be an "inequitable" failure to cooperate with the school district. The last thing you want is to have a winning case that you then lose because you inadvertently shoot yourself in the foot.[41]

---

41 The threat of this happening is not merely theoretical. Some years ago, we had a client relocate with her children to the New York area after living for several years in a Southern state. After a weeklong hearing, we won several hundred thousand dollars in reimbursement relief. However, the trial judge then cut that award *in half* because the school district was able to show that, before we were ever engaged as counsel, the student's mother had withheld reports written by the Southern school district as part of the IEP development process. Had these reports been shared, they might have made a difference in the new school district's decision-making. When a parent engages in conduct that a judge might consider "inequitable," it exposes the parent to the risk of serious adverse consequences.

If you have secured any private assessments or evaluations, it can be critical to make sure that these reports are shared with the school district, at or preferably before the IEP meeting. Doing so can also help to change the dynamic from "this is what the parents want" to "this is what professionals are recommending." It is worth repeating that it is far easier for school districts to follow the written evaluation and recommendations of a professional rather than simply capitulate to a parental request. For this reason, if parents can afford it, a comprehensive private evaluation that comes with recommendations can be extremely valuable.

Choosing the Appropriate IEP Classification

Once the available evaluations are reviewed and it is apparent that a school-aged student meets the threshold eligibility requirements, the IEP team is required to consider the student's administrative classification for purposes of the IEP.[42] In many cases, a parent will choose or advocate for an autism classification, and for good reason. It is important to choose autism if that is the accurate classification[43] because that classification can lay the groundwork for far greater service levels than might otherwise be denied to a student with a different diagnosis.

I think that parents often make a terrible mistake when they resist the classification of autism, believing that applying that label will stigmatize their child and sabotage their chances of going to college or finding a marriage partner. The reality is that today, many students on the autism spectrum will attend college or a post-graduate experience and have fulfilling personal lives.

These days, using a college application essay as a platform to share the story of a student's autism and its impact might actually *enhance* the chances of being accepted at a school of their choice. And in addition to the popular dating sites for the neurotypical population, there are now a number of dating sites specifically for people who are on the spectrum. Today, there is far less stigma for individuals who disclose being on the autism spectrum.[44]

---

42 Preschool students are not required to be designated under any specific classification. In New York State, for example, a preschool student eligible to receive special education services is generically classified as a "preschooler with a disability."

43 Sometimes there are comorbid medical conditions (e.g. epilepsy, life-threatening allergies, etc.) that, coupled with the student's autism diagnosis, will support the classification of "Other Health Impaired" (OHI). Many IEP teams will grapple with the task of weighing and reconciling these two administrative classifications.

44 The comedian and actor Amy Schumer, for example, proudly proclaims that she is married to a man who is on the spectrum.

Developing Behavior Plans

There are, of course, a broad range of behaviors that might interfere with a student's learning or the learning of other students. Some school districts will make the mistake of guessing at putting together an appropriate behavior plan without first exercising the requisite due diligence. According to Dr. Amy Davies-Lackey, Education Director of the Manhattan Childrens Center, "The development of behavior intervention plans is a data-driven process. After first identifying the target behaviors, data should be taken on the frequency and duration of those behaviors and what environmental conditions were present. That information is needed to determine the likely *function* of the target behavior. Without doing that homework, you're just guessing."

Developing Ambitious and Challenging IEP Goals

Today's parents have the right under the *Endrew F.* decision to insist that IEP goals and objectives be sufficiently ambitious and challenging in relation to the student's unique needs and potential. To meet that standard, it is incumbent upon school districts to "baseline" test students to ascertain what they already have mastered and what continues to represent a challenge. And, when the school district proposes goals and objectives for inclusion in the student's IEP, parents need to be vigilant, identifying and objecting to any goals that would likely *not* be challenging ("Oh, he can already do that"). Finally, it is incumbent upon school districts to collect data as to how the student progresses with his or her IEP goals. Otherwise, when next year's IEP review meeting comes rolling around, no one will have a clue about how to propose genuinely challenging goals and objectives for the following school year.

Developing IEP Goals That Address ADL Skills

There are many "activities of daily living" that warrant the development of IEP goals written to be implemented *after* school. This is particularly the case with toileting, dressing and undressing, hygiene issues, paying with cash or a credit card and learning to cross safely at a crosswalk. These kinds of skills may be quite difficult to address in a school building environment.

Developing IEP Goals To Address And Build COVID-19 Safety Skills

Today's students will need to learn and become comfortable with additional safety measures. They will likely need to learn how and when to don and remove a face mask or gloves, maintaining an appropriate distance between themselves and others, and how to identify symptoms that they may need to bring to the attention of a teacher, parent or other caregiver. We have to adapt to today's realities, painful as they may be. These kinds of health and safety goals currently need to be built into the student's IEP as part of addressing "activities of daily living" (ADL).

Managing and Fading Prompting Levels

It is a serious problem when reliance on prompting is *assumed* within the IEP without further conditions or limitations. To promote greater levels of independence, the use of the "prompt hierarchy" has to be proactively managed within the four corners of the IEP plan. Dr. Ivy Feldman, Executive Director of the Keswell School in Manhattan, provides the following example: "In the beginning, the IEP might state 'with hand-over-hand prompting, Mark will learn to tie his shoes.' Based on Mark's progress, you want to build in efforts to *fade* and reduce that level of prompting so that Mark can display the skill without needing hand-over-hand assistance. At the other end of the prompt hierarchy, the IEP goal for this skill might be 'Mark will put on and tie his shoes when requested to do so.' Or, even better, 'Mark will put on and tie his shoes independently, without any prompting, as part of getting dressed for the day.'"

Making a Case for Reasonable Accommodations and Other Classroom Supports

Placing a student in the "right" classroom is always a good start, but additional supports may need to be implemented. Many students with autism will need some additional accommodations and classroom supports to be successful—particularly when they are placed in an inclusion setting or are trying to learn in a crowded classroom with many other students.[45] Many of these accommodations and related classroom supports will be directly related to the student's learning style and distractibility. Examples of additional classroom supports and accommodations that might be appropriate for inclusion on the IEP include:

- ✓ One-on-one teaching support
- ✓ Proximate seating (closer to teacher)
- ✓ Maintaining appropriate "social distance"
- ✓ Additional time to take tests or to turn in work
- ✓ Quiet, non-distractible environment for test-taking
- ✓ FM Unit (amplifying teacher's voice while screening out background noise)
- ✓ Sensory breaks
- ✓ Access to computer keyboard or other assistive technology

---

[45] The COVID-19 pandemic is likely to force significant changes in the configuration of classrooms that will modify, if not eliminate, the crowded classrooms of yesteryear.

- ✓ Advance notice of teacher's lesson plans
- ✓ Ready access to classroom notes recorded by a designated notetaker
- ✓ Additional set of textbooks for use at home

It is always better if parents come to the IEP meeting armed with evaluations that expressly recommend specific accommodations and related classroom supports that the student needs. Need is the determining factor, not simply that the support being requested would be helpful or make things "better."

Maximizing Access to the Regular Curriculum

The federal IDEA statute contains only a handful of "maximizing" provisions. One of the best-known maximizing provisions (discussed in Chapter 4, page 43) is the statutory mandate to educate students in their "least restrictive environment." It is Congress' preference that students be educated in their least restrictive environment, even if that requires implementing additional supports and aids. When students with autism are being educated in a mainstream or inclusion setting, it is almost always necessary to implement some additional supports.

The statute contains the same kind of maximizing language by mandating a student's access to the regular curriculum to the "maximum extent appropriate." By using the phrase "maximum *extent*," Congress has communicated its understanding that every student's ability to access the regular curriculum will differ in terms of degree.

Some school districts will resist implementing the regular curriculum unless the student can display the prerequisite skills to operate *exclusively* within that curriculum. For these school districts, accessing the regular curriculum is something that must be earned. However, that is an errant, inflexible, and inappropriate approach that fails to follow the intent of the statute. Access to the regular curriculum is not an all or nothing proposition and does not need to be earned. The truth is that with appropriate *modifications* based on the student's unique presentment, the regular curriculum is scalable.

Asking a school district to commit to modifying the general curriculum for a student can sometimes be met with significant resistance by teachers and administrators. Modifying the general curriculum normally requires significant periodic investments of time and attention. Just as an ill-fitting suit may require hours of tailoring to fit, there is no magic wand to modify the regular curriculum. The regular curriculum is very much tied to greater independence. Accordingly, in cases where accessing the regular education curriculum is appropriate and would benefit the student, parents and their advocates should not hesitate to press the school district to modify the regular curriculum so that it can become accessible to the student.

The Importance of Putting Extracurricular Activities on the IEP

A student with an IEP is just as eligible for field trips, afterschool clubs, and sports participation as a student without one. Extracurricular activities can represent valuable opportunities and steps toward greater independence and self-esteem. Whenever possible, and provided that the activity is within the bounds of public health and safety, parents should include these extracurricular activities (and any related goals and objectives that are developed for those activities) as mandates in the student's IEP.

Several years ago, we were contacted by the family of Anthony Starego, a talented football placekicker diagnosed with autism. Due to his age, Anthony was deemed ineligible under New Jersey high school athletic association rules to kick during his senior year. Anthony's high school in New Jersey could not have been more supportive, as were his teammates. Anthony and his parents asked us to bring a federal court action to secure one final season for Anthony to be able to kick for the team that he loved.

Anthony's high school football team, the Green Dragons, had a longstanding history of not doing very well in the standings. The Green Dragons' win-loss record hardly represented a threat to any of the competitive high school football teams. Accordingly, we were able to represent to the Court and to the New Jersey athletic association that if Anthony was allowed to play for one final season, he was not likely to be a "difference maker." His team's anemic and unimpressive record gave us good grounds to ask, "What possible harm is going to occur if Anthony is allowed to kick for just one more season?"

Two games into the season, we were able to reach a settlement with the New Jersey athletic association allowing Anthony to kick for the remaining games. Anthony and his parents were ecstatic. Anthony's teammates were elated to hear the good news. In fact, Anthony's team was so inspired by this development that, with Anthony's kicking help, the Green Dragons went on that year to *win* the State Championship.[46]

Extracurricular activities are not just for the "regular" students. The importance of these activities to promote greater levels of independence and self-esteem cannot be overstated.

---

[46] To see Anthony Starego's exceptional kicking skills in action, see ESPN's You-Tube video treatment entitled "The Kick of Hope."

The Talented Anthony Starego

The School District's Obligation to Consider Parental Requests In Good Faith

In Chapter 1, I discussed the outcome of the *Deal* case where the Hamilton County, Tennessee school system refused to *consider* the parents' request to fund their son's ABA program. The consequence of this refusal was quite severe, as the Court awarded the Deal family tuition reimbursement relief as well as statutory costs and attorneys' fees. The *Deal* case was one of the very first federal court decisions to recognize that *predetermination* by the school system is impermissible.

How Parents Should Address Concerns About Bullying at the IEP Level

While the *Deal* case involved a claim of "predetermination" where the issue was funding for an ABA program, the Second Circuit's landmark decision in *T.K. v. NYCDOE* saw the same principles applied when parents repeatedly attempted to discuss the bullying that their daughter was enduring in her public elementary school classroom at PS 6, located in Manhattan.

The student's parents had repeatedly tried to discuss the bullying problem without success. Whenever the request was made (at IEP meetings or other meetings held in the principal's office), the parents were told that it was neither the time nor the place to have such a discussion—and were never offered an appropriate time or a place to do so.

The New York City Department of Education refused to have any discussion about bullying or the below drawing—a drawing that reveals the hostile environment that was allowed to exist in this student's classroom. The drawing refers to the student with derogatory, self-esteem crushing language including "ugly hair," "nose picking," "ugly smile," "fat ass" and "bad body."[47] The classroom teacher apparently picked up the drawing and threw it into the trash. Thanks to the student's alert classroom aide, the drawing was rescued from the trash and delivered to the student's parents so they would have some physical evidence to counter the school's position that there was "no bullying" going on at PS 6.

The classroom teacher was only making things worse for the student, making her feel like a pariah. When the student's classmates complained that a certain pencil in the classroom had been "touched" by the student, the teacher's counterproductive response was to "mark" the pencil with the student's name so that there would be no chance of anyone else coming into physical contact with the student's pencil. In this manner, the classroom teacher *reinforced* the stigmatizing and hurtful behavior of the student's classmates. The classroom teacher was essentially communicating to her entire class that it was acceptable to treat this student as an outcast.

---

[47] The drawing that appears on page 70 is redacted only for purposes of protecting the student's identity. The lawsuit used only initials in identifying the student and her parents.

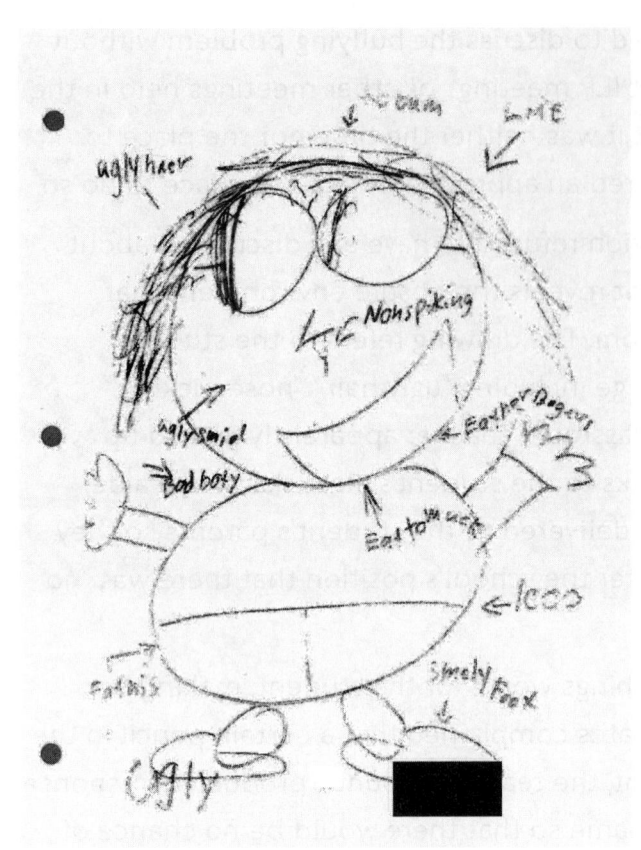

The Derogatory Drawing PS 6
Administrators Refused to Discuss

The bullying problem was all but guaranteed to continue given PS 6's administrators' refusal to even discuss it. The student's parents could not imagine returning their daughter to PS 6 under those circumstances. Accordingly, they withdrew their daughter from PS 6 and placed her in a private, therapeutic, state-approved school costing approximately $30,000 per year.

Even after the case arrived at the federal appeal stage, it continued to be New York City's position that the student had not been bullied.

PS 6's Principal, Lauren Fontana, had to be ordered by the federal court to appear for deposition. When I asked Ms. Fontana, under oath, about the existence of roughly a half dozen "incident reports" that the student's parents had requested, but which had not been timely provided, Ms. Fontana referred to the incident reports, on the record, as "the f***ing incident reports." In my opinion, by using such language on the record, Ms. Fontana was openly thumbing her nose at the student's parents and the entire court process. I would like to think that pretty much any other elementary school principal would have chosen different language. In any event, Ms. Fontana's glib and offensive testimony spoke volumes as to how it was possible that Ms. Fontana repeatedly refused to discuss the bullying issue with L.K.'s parents.

The federal district court judge assigned to the case was the legendary Hon. Jack Weinstein.[48] After a mini-trial (and despite New York City's prior protests to the contrary), Judge Weinstein ruled that the student had been *repeatedly* bullied while at PS 6 and that just as in the *Deal* case, New York City's school administrators had improperly refused to consider or discuss the parents' concerns.

New York City elected to take a further appeal to the Second Circuit Court of Appeals. All this did was delay the ultimate day of reckoning. It also gave the United States Department of Justice the opportunity to intervene and support the student's position.

The Second Circuit agreed with Judge Weinstein that the student had been repeatedly bullied while at PS 6 and that New York City had improperly excluded the student's parents from the IEP development process by flatly refusing to discuss the bullying issue. As the Court of Appeals ruled: "We conclude that the [NYCDOE] denied L.K. a FAPE by violating her parents' procedural right to participate in the development of the IEP. At two separate meetings... plaintiffs sought to discuss L.K.'s bullying, but school officials *refused* to do so."

New York City was ordered to reimburse the cost of L.K.'s private-school tuition.[49] In addition, New York City was obligated to pay the student's substantial attorneys' fees over an almost eight-year time frame involving four separate court levels. The legal takeaway from the *T.K.* case is that school districts are legally obligated to give due consideration to concerns a parent might raise for discussion. When a school district gives parents the cold shoulder in response to their requests for discussion and consideration, that school district might be doing so at their peril.

To properly address suspected bullying at the IEP stage, parents should consider the following:

- ✓ Request (in writing) any "incident reports" referring to your child—teachers sometimes provide incident reports to school administrators that are not shared with parents
- ✓ Request a meeting or phone call with the classroom teacher to ascertain what he or

---

48 Until his retirement this year at 98, Judge Weinstein continued to display the productivity and energy level of someone half his age. Many years ago, Judge Weinstein was one of Ruth Bader Ginsburg's law professors at Columbia Law School (after Justice Ginsburg had transferred from Harvard). He also is known for drafting many of the briefs filed in the landmark civil rights case, *Brown v. Board of Education*.

49 The private school that L.K.'s parents sent her to was state-approved. Given that status, New York City could have had the tuition paid for by New York State had it only approved L.K.'s transfer. New York City missed that golden opportunity—much as it missed the opportunity to address (and acknowledge) the bullying problem at PS 6 when L.K.'s parents attempted to raise the issue.

she may be seeing

- ✓ Try to speak with the classroom aide
- ✓ Engage an educational consultant do a classroom/lunch/recess observation
- ✓ Request a special IEP meeting to discuss the problem
- ✓ Consider the development of IEP goals that will help mitigate the situation
- ✓ Identify and isolate the bully (as opposed to your child, the victim, being moved to another class, having lunch in a separate location, etc.)

Communicating and Documenting Disagreement—Without Being Disagreeable

The IEP meeting normally takes place in a school building or administrative office. When disagreements arise (and they will), it is important to be able to *disagree without being disagreeable.* You don't want to be known to the school district as the "nightmare parent" and you certainly don't want a hearing officer coming to that conclusion either. Just as you are about to press the "send" button, ask yourself how a hearing officer would likely react to what you just wrote.[50] Similarly, whether you are on the phone or at an IEP meeting, act as if everything you say is being recorded or transcribed. As with so many disputes, it's not so much what you say, but rather *how* you say it.

When push comes to shove, a parent might win at due process but cannot win at the IEP meeting. After all, the IEP meeting is held on the school district's home turf and is very much under school district control. Nor will a parent win by rushing through the IEP development process as if they were a contestant on *Jeopardy*. Take your time in identifying those aspects of the IEP that you don't agree with. Don't let school district administrators pressure you into an immediate decision you may later regret. If the process needs another meeting, so be it. Pick your battles.[51] Consider speaking with counsel or with an educational consultant.

Always Focus on Your Child's Needs

When you make your record, the theme should be your child's documented *needs*, not a wish list of what might be "best." Ideally, your child's needs will be revealed during the course of assessments—which will help you change the dynamic from "this is what the parent wants" to the much more persuasive "this is what the professionals recommend."

---

50 Another hot tip from *L.K. v. NYCDOE*: If you are called to testify under oath, whatever you do, do not use the "f" word in any of its many permutations.

51 School district administrators roll their eyes when they speak of the kind of parents who "never met an issue that they didn't like." For this reason, it is important for parents to pick their battles.

It is important to receive a copy of the proposed IEP to make a proper record. Some school districts such as New York City will prepare and send out the resulting IEP document days or weeks after the IEP meeting. In that scenario, parents should press for a copy of the proposed IEP.[52] Unless the parents' claim is that the school district failed to provide them with an IEP, it is important that the school district's IEP position be memorialized in writing before challenging the school district's decision-making.

What are the Differences Between an IEP and a Section 504 Plan?

While there always will be exceptions, in general I find that most students who are on the autism spectrum will qualify for and need an Individualized Education Plan (IEP) as opposed to a Section 504 Plan. Here are the salient differences between the two plans.

The entitlement to an IEP arises under the federal IDEA statute and makes provision for a written special education plan, provided that the student fits under an eligible category of disability and that disability has an adverse impact on the student's educational performance and/or ability to learn. While Section 504 plans are often in writing, they don't have to be. They arise under Section 504 of the Rehabilitation Act and they are all about ensuring *access* to learning opportunities at school. It is quite a bit easier to qualify for a Section 504 Plan than a full-blown IEP. All that needs to be shown is the presence of a disability, or a learning or attentional issue that interferes with the student's ability to learn.

Typically, a student's IEP team will consist of the student's parent or guardian, a special education teacher, a regular education teacher, a school psychologist, and the school district's designated representative. The Section 504 team, on the other hand, need only include a handful of people who are "familiar" with the student. It normally is sufficient if parents, a teacher, and the school principal are in attendance at the Section 504 team meeting.

The IEP is intended to be far more comprehensive and will cover the student's present levels of performance; the development of goals and objectives; the scope and timing of services, accommodations, and modifications; participation in standardized assessments; eligibility for summer services; transition support; and how (if at all) the student will be included in general education classes. The 504 Plan, on the other hand,

---

[52] A parent waiting to receive a copy of the IEP might write to the school district as follows: "The IEP meeting for my child was held on [date]. To date, however, we still have not received a copy of the proposed IEP. Please advise." Even the simplest email or letter faxed to the school district makes a better record than the phone call you will most certainly lose track of.

will cover the issue of accommodations that the student might need and identify the names and functions of the individuals responsible for implementing the plan. For example, a Section 504 Plan might make provision for a student with Type I Diabetes who must rely on an insulin pump to receive support from the school nurse.

In the IEP development process, as discussed in Chapter 5 (page 51), parents have the right to request an independent evaluation at school district expense. The Section 504 Plan route has no corresponding entitlement for an independent evaluation. If the student ever needs an independent evaluation that the parent cannot afford to pay for, this distinction can create a serious problem. Good reasons, then, to press for an IEP when warranted—or if the situation is a close call.

If the school district intends to make any changes to the IEP, it must provide the student's parent or guardian with "prior written notice" and normally must also reconvene the IEP team to discuss the proposed changes. The Section 504 team is required to notify a student's family if there are to be any "significant" changes, but the notification is not required to be in writing (i.e. the notification might consist of a voicemail message). Federal IDEA funds are available to help support IEP development and implementation, but they are not available for the development or implementation of Section 504 Plans.

A Section 504 Plan might suffice for students who are lightly impacted and merely require some basic accommodations to be successful in school. However, given that even most "higher functioning" students on the autism spectrum will require far more in terms of services and related protections, pursuing eligibility for a comprehensive IEP is usually the more prudent path to take. Parents should take care not to be seduced into pursuing a Section 504 Plan simply because such plans are easier to qualify for.

Chapter 7
Considering Claims Against School Districts—
What Relief Is Available?

We regularly receive calls from parents at the end of their rope who will ask us to determine whether (and to what extent) they might have viable claims to assert against their child's school district. While there are many viable potential claims, certain measures some parents may wish to pursue are simply not viable as claims. Or, a claim might need to await the "exhaustion" of available administrative remedies.[53]

For example, your child's classroom teacher might be excellent—or incompetent, burnt out, or otherwise lacking the skills and experience to work with a particular child. While the IDEA statute empowers hearing officers and federal judges to exercise a great deal of power, firing the classroom teacher or denying the teacher tenure or their pension are not matters within the court's jurisdiction.

There are many other requests that similarly do not fall within a court's jurisdiction. No hearing officer or judge can direct a school district to build a specialized school that a parent might want to see "in-district." Nor can they order a school district to hire certain personnel that a parent requests for their child or order a school district to permit privately paid teachers to support a student in the public school classroom. Attorneys cannot win monetary damages based on the parent's emotional distress

---

[53] For example, assume that a parent thinking about suing their child's school district has two claims to assert. The first claim is that the school district's improper use of restraint procedures resulted in the student's arm being broken. The second claim is that for months, the child's weekly speech therapy mandate on their IEP went unfulfilled. In this scenario, depending on how the claims are brought, it is possible that the personal injury claim for the broken arm may have to await the adjudication of the "administrative" claim (that the student did not receive their speech mandate). It is essential to discuss these kinds of procedural issues with counsel so that you do not inadvertently assert a claim that might be dismissed for failing to exhaust available administrative remedies.

resulting from seeing their child languish or regress in an inadequate educational program. The above scenarios are never going to be the subject of a judicial mandate.

Depending on the supporting facts, without limitation, viable claims at the administrative level might include:

- ✓ Tuition funding claims (including reimbursement and direct payment)
- ✓ Compensatory education claims
- ✓ Claims challenging the student's IEP classification
- ✓ Claims challenging the school district's failure to declare the student eligible for services
- ✓ Claims seeking reimbursement for an independent evaluation
- ✓ Claims challenging the adequacy or appropriateness of IEP goals
- ✓ Claims seeking additional classroom supports or accommodations
- ✓ Claims designed to ensure the student's safe access to an education
- ✓ Claims concerning the student's transportation supports
- ✓ Claims concerning the student's eligibility for ESY (Summer) services
- ✓ Claims challenging school placements as inadequate or inappropriate
- ✓ Claims to enforce IEP mandates not being fulfilled
- ✓ Claims to gain access to assistive technology/augmentive communication
- ✓ Claims to conduct additional assessments and evaluations

Can The COVID-19 Pandemic Give Rise To Any Claims?

In view of the public health and safety concerns associated with the potential for virus transmission during an ongoing pandemic, it appears that parents now have an additional claim to raise if, for example, the school district offers the student an unduly crowded and congested classroom or otherwise fail to observe and maintain responsible social distancing. The argument to be made is that safe access to an appropriate education is an integral component of the right to a free and appropriate public education.

The Requirement to Send a "10-Day Letter"

In general, parents who believe that their school system should pay for private schools and other services are under an affirmative obligation to put the school system *on notice* of this claim at least 10 school days before implementing the private program. While there is no express requirement that the 10-day notice be sent by legal counsel, the prudent parent should consult with counsel beforehand. Why? Because if the parent fails to send the notice properly, if is sent to the wrong recipient, or the notice does not "cover" all the items being reserved for a claim, such failures can impair or even preclude an intended claim.[54] With so much at stake, parents who send their own 10-day notice may be risking everything.

On the next page is an example of what a 10-day letter might look like in a situation where the parent concludes that the school district has failed to offer adequate speech and language therapy. Bear in mind that the 10-day notice letter is something that needs to be sent to an appropriate school district *administrator*, not to your child's teacher or classroom aide:

---

[54] Notice can also be given at an IEP meeting and the notice requirement might not even apply in extreme circumstances where a student is being removed from a genuine zone of danger. Given all the many permutations, parents should consult with counsel as to how to best handle a 10-day notice situation.

Dr. Barbara Weston, Director of Special Services
Mastrich Central School District
Youngstown, Ohio

Dear Dr. Weston:

Thank you for reconvening Michael's IEP so that we could discuss the significance of the most recent speech and language evaluation.

The latest evaluation shows that Michael is not receiving nearly enough speech and language therapy from the district. Although the evaluation concludes that our son needs to be receiving at least four hours of one-to-one speech and language therapy each week, you communicated that because of this year's budget and "staffing difficulties," the district is not in a position to increase Michael's speech mandate above the half-hour per week "group" session reflected in the current IEP.

Under the circumstances, please be advised that after ten days,[55] and going forward for the balance of this school year, we intend to secure the additional speech and language therapy recommended in the evaluation and that we will be looking to the district to pay for such services.

Please make sure to place a copy of this letter in our son's permanent educational record. Thank you.

Roberta Koenig

As noted above, sending a 10-day letter (and reviewing any response by the school district) is a critical procedural juncture that warrants consultation with an attorney.

---

55 Not counting weekends or holidays.

Chapter 8
When All Else Fails—Filing For an Impartial Hearing (Due Process)

While many disputes can be resolved at the IEP meeting level or following the receipt of a 10-day notice letter, others will remain unresolved in anticipation of a formal due process challenge known as an "impartial hearing." Parents should be aware that under the federal IDEA statute, there is (in most cases) a strict two-year statute of limitations applicable to filing claims.[56] Moreover, while parents sometimes learn of additional violations and claims *after* filing for due process, a hearing officer normally can only adjudicate the claims expressly alleged in the parent's due process complaint—unless the parent's due process complaint can be amended as of right or the school district "opens the door" to the additional claim.[57]

Memories fade. Letters and other communications can be lost. Witnesses move or take other employment. The takeaway here is that parents should file for due process when claims are relatively fresh, making sure that all claims are expressly stated within the four corners of the due process filing. Parents won't get any credit for holding back.

Sometimes, it is crystal clear that the school district is in the wrong. If, for example, the district forgets to schedule the student's IEP meeting and the new school year starts without a current IEP, it probably would not be a case that the school district will want to litigate. Nor will a school district attempt to defend a situation where a student with autism with perfectly good hearing is recommended for placement at a school for the

---

[56] There are circumstances that may operate to "toll" (temporarily suspend) the statute of limitations, but parents should not assume, without consulting with an attorney, that they can toll the statute. Parents should assume that a two-year limitation will apply.
[57] Some courts have held that a hearing officer may adjudicate issues that are not expressly pleaded by a parent if the school district has "opened the door" to the issue. This entails a complicated exception to the pleading requirement that warrants consultation with counsel.

deaf—which actually happened to one of our client families. I don't know how such monumental goofs arise, except to note that while parents are "case managers" for a single student (their own child), the school district is trying to manage IEP development for many students, often in a compressed and rushed timeframe.

Litigating a Case Against the District's "Teacher of the Year"

The dispute between a student's parents and the school district can sometimes be an honest, "gray area" dispute that can only be resolved at a hearing. I once tried a case in Westchester County, New York where our client was seeking tuition reimbursement for their daughter's attendance at a well-known private school. Our client presented with a variety of learning challenges, as well as a serious auditory processing disorder.

The student's parents were emphatic that their school district was not ready, willing, or able to educate their daughter. The school district was equally adamant that it was offering a great program and a great teacher. As proof of the classroom teacher's unique level of expertise, the school district's counsel let me in on a little secret he planned to unleash during the hearing: The teacher in question had just been recognized as New York State's "Teacher of The Year." The school district's attorney asked me the same question I was asking myself: "How are you ever going to get past 'teacher of the year'?"

The case went to hearing with this excellent teacher being called as the school district's first witness. The teacher came off exactly as advertised: Brilliant, articulate, compassionate, well-informed, highly trained, a "teacher's teacher," a true professional. Yet, perhaps with a bit of divine intervention, the teacher's direct testimony revealed a serious, if not insurmountable, flaw.

At least five times during the teacher's direct testimony, the court reporter stopped recording the teacher's words, picked up her hands, and complained on the record that the teacher was speaking too fast for her testimony to be transcribed. After the fifth time this happened, the hearing officer, on the record, asked the teacher to please slow down so that her testimony could be taken down by the court reporter. The teacher promised to do better but within minutes, the court reporter was complaining again that the teacher was speaking too fast for her to take down her words.

When I cross-examined the teacher, the first thing I did was congratulate her for being recognized as teacher of the year. I then asked how she planned to teach this student, with her auditory processing disorder. The teacher explained that it would be no problem since she would "naturally" adjust the speed and presentation of her language to accommodate the student's auditory processing challenges. "Really?" I asked. "How are you going to 'naturally' adjust the speed of your words when you were not able to do so even after repeatedly being asked by the court reporter and the hearing officer to slow down?" The teacher's candid response? "That's a good question."

It was a good question—one that was good enough to win the case. The school district was offering the student an excellent teacher on paper. However, that teacher's rapid-fire presentation made her a poor match for our client's auditory processing challenges.

Do Parents Always Need to Hire Counsel to File for Due Process?

Is an attorney always necessary, or would a non-attorney advocate suffice? The answer depends on a number of considerations. If, for example, the claim is straightforward enough or the amount in controversy is close to what it would cost to engage counsel, it might be appropriate and economical to proceed *pro se* or with a non-attorney advocate. But there are many more claims that do need the support of experienced counsel. When the objective is to recover reimbursement for the $100,000-plus tuition you were forced to borrow from your 401(k) savings, it's probably not the time to take the risk of going it alone. At the end of the day, nobody wants to have to report "Honey, I lost our child's case."

Preserving and Invoking Your Child's "Pendency" Entitlements

There often is a lot of confusion about the statutory right of "pendency" (sometimes referred to as "stay put"). Pendency is designed to maintain the educational status quo while the due process proceedings are pending, until there is a "final" decision. A parent does not "file for pendency" per se. Rather, pendency is an ancillary right and protection that, once properly invoked, supports the parent's other claims. While pendency is an unconditional and automatic right, it is a right than can only be *triggered* and invoked by filing for due process. Without that filing, there is no obligation on the part of the school district to honor the student's pendency entitlements.

Assume, for example, that a six-year-old student living in Ardsley, New York has an IEP requiring 30 hours per week of 1:1 instruction, speech therapy, occupational therapy, and physical therapy. This student's family moves to a neighboring school district within New York State that proposes substantial cuts in the student's IEP services—cuts that the parents do not wish to accept. The student's parents could file for due process in the new school district and invoke the student's pendency entitlements. Under this scenario, until the due process proceeding is finally adjudicated, the new school district is obliged to continue to honor and perform the mandates enumerated in the Ardsley IEP.

When pendency is invoked, can a parent count on being reimbursed for the money paid for the parent's chosen providers? It depends. In New York City, for example, the school system normally allows parents to continue using their chosen providers for pendency purposes. Some suburban school systems, however, will respond to a parent's invocation of pendency by offering providers selected by the school district. When the district offers to perform pendency with its chosen providers, a parent takes a significant risk by refusing the district's offer.[58] The parent who refuses to use these providers assumes the risk of not being able to recoup pendency expenses incurred after the school district offered the pendency providers.[59]

What happens if my child's pendency placement goes out of business? Pendency is rooted in the student's last agreed upon placement and program. However, pendency is not a specific place, nor a specific service provider. Sometimes, a child's pendency placement will go out of business, be destroyed in a flood or fire, or simply not be available.[60] When that happens, the parent and the school district should work together to locate a "substantially similar" program. If the school district fails to cooperate on that point, a hearing officer or judge can order the school district to honor pendency by funding a substantially similar alternative placement.[61]

While pendency is a right that can move with the student *within* the state where the student resides (i.e. from one in-state school district to another), there is no pendency entitlement that travels with the student moving to another state. And except in certain states like New Jersey, pendency is not recognized for students moving from "early intervention" programs to programming available for students who are turning three. In the above cases, the "new" IEP is likely to become the student's pendency entitlement.

Settlement Considerations

Filing a demand for due process automatically triggers a 30-day "resolution"

---

58 If the school district offers personnel who will be providing the pendency services, parents can probe the bona fides of such an offer by asking for a proposed schedule with the names and functions of the school district's providers. A school district that is ready, willing, and able to itself perform the pendency services should have no difficulty responding to such a request.

59 See *T.M. et al. v. Cornwall Central School District* (2d Circuit 2014).

60 This happened throughout the State of Louisiana following Hurricane Katrina.

61 In *P.M. v. NYCDOE*, the student's pendency placement was a school named AMAC, which offered an ABA-based program and related services. Unfortunately, AMAC went bankrupt and was no longer available to serve as the student's pendency placement. The school district did not offer or identify any placement or program as being the student's pendency placement. The hearing officer ruled that the school district, under pendency, would be required to fund the student's placement at the Keswell School, based upon the hearing officer's finding that the Keswell School's ABA-based program was "substantially similar" to AMAC's (defunct) program.

period—a period of time when the school district has the opportunity to meet with parents at a "resolution meeting" to ascertain if the claims can be settled without the need for a formal adjudication from a hearing officer. If the case can be settled, the school district's primary incentives are saving time and money, avoiding the risk of setting bad precedent, and the fact that by settling, the parent will have no legal right to recover attorneys' fees or other costs. The parents' settlement considerations might include, among other factors:

- ✓ Mitigating the risk of a loss at trial
- ✓ Accelerating the recovery of program costs
- ✓ Conserving the expenditure of attorneys' fees
- ✓ Conserving additional expert witness fees
- ✓ Conserving the time needed to prepare for a hearing
- ✓ Freeing up workdays that otherwise would be needed for the hearing
- ✓ The certainty of the settlement benefits
- ✓ Reducing personal/family anxiety and stress
- ✓ Avoiding any time-consuming and costly appeals
- ✓ Preserving the student's pendency entitlements in the event of a future dispute
- ✓ Promoting good relations with school district personnel

Parents often ask, "What do you think would be a good settlement for my case?" Or, they may be aware of another family's settlement package and wonder if that identical result can be achieved in their case. Just as an appropriate education plan needs to be tailored to meet the unique needs of the student, the value of any proposed settlement must be measured on a case-by-case basis against the family's stated objectives, the likelihood of success, the family's ability to fund the student's program, and the family's tolerance for risk. Good settlements are built from the ground up by making a solid record from the start and by preparing to go to hearing in way that's visible and lets the school district's attorney know you mean business.

Why Multi-Year Settlements Should Always Be Reviewed by Counsel

Some school districts will offer parents a multi-year settlement agreement. While genuine multi-year settlements can be quite valuable for families looking to plan ahead budget-wise, they can turn problematic if the child's needs go in a direction not addressed by the settlement agreement. You don't want to be locked into a situation where flexibility would have offered more value. Multi-year settlements can also be problematic if the parents are locked in but the school district is not, making the "multi-year" feature illusory. If a multi-year settlement is on the table for discussion, it should be reviewed by counsel; there should be a full discussion of the risks of proceeding.

The "Unsigning Bonus"

School districts may not admit this, but they do not exactly celebrate when autism families arrive from other school districts. When a new autism family moves into the district, it sets into motion many hours of administrative work and places additional financial and personnel burdens on the school district. Some districts see these situations as a countdown to an expensive residential placement. Truth be told, if they were permitted to do so, it is my sense that many school districts would openly compensate autism families if they would agree to move elsewhere. In the film *An Officer and A Gentleman*, drill sergeant Emil Foley (Louis Gossett, Jr.) presses Zack Mayo (Richard Gere) to quit his quest to become a Navy pilot. Mayo's response is that he has "nowhere else to go." Many families find themselves in the same position—they may have little choice but to stand and fight.

Sometimes, however, families litigating due process cases with their school districts will consider moving to another district just to get a fresh start. If your family is on the fence about moving—and you are in the middle of settlement discussions that have not yet reached a solution—you or your counsel may consider using the prospect of moving out of district by a certain date as leverage to reach an acceptable settlement level. This "unsigning bonus" is a very sensitive proposal that normally requires the assistance of experienced counsel.

The Right to Recover Attorneys' Fees as a "Prevailing Party"

When parents and counsel win a significant victory in a hearing and emerge from the process (and any timely appeals) as the "prevailing" party, parents have the right under the IDEA statute to make an application in federal court to be awarded reasonable attorneys' fees and costs.[62] The purpose of this fee-shifting provision in the statute is to give parents a financial incentive to hire competent counsel to vindicate their children's rights to a free and appropriate public education (FAPE).

Most of these fee claims will be settled out of court. If the fee claim is not settled, the court's fee award will be predicated on a review of the attorney's contemporaneous

---

[62] While the U.S. Supreme Court has ruled in the *Buckhannon* case that there is no legal right to recover attorneys' fees based on a mere settlement agreement, it is possible to recover fees if the settlement agreement is reached and "so ordered" under the express auspices of the federal court (i.e. the court acted to reorder the rights of the parties).

billing records, the attorney's expertise and years of experience, the difficulty and complexity of the subject matter, the relief that was achieved, and a variety of other recognized factors.

Rarely, however, are attorneys' fees awarded at 100% of the attorneys' billing records: Courts often impose cuts for one reason or another. If, for example, a parent wins only a miniscule portion of the requested relief, the reviewing court will likely impose a fee cut that recognizes this differential. The reviewing court also may deduct hours if the record shows that there were excessive numbers of attorneys on the case, or that work was done by highly experienced lawyers that could easily have been done at paralegal rates. The reviewing court may also disallow hours performed by an attorney who also happens to be the student's parent.

In addition to anticipated cuts, it can be many months (or even longer) before the court decides the fee application. Accordingly, if the school district makes a solid offer on fees, parents have every incentive *not* to hold out for the last dollar. Parents should focus their attention on the sandcastle, not the individual grains of sand.

The mere threat of having to pay for the parents' attorneys' fees and costs (on top of having to pay fees to the school district's attorneys) is a sufficiently powerful incentive for school districts to resolve disputes *before* they have to be formally adjudicated by a hearing officer. While there is no legal right to recover attorneys' fees in situations where there is a private settlement between the parties, some school systems will still pay *some* amount for attorneys' fees. It never hurts to ask!

When the School District Makes an "Offer of Judgment"

As noted above, the 30-day "resolution period" following the due process filing provides an opportunity to parents and school districts alike to resolve conflicts early on, when the parties are less likely to be entrenched in their respective positions.

Parents who file for due process and are hoping for an award of attorneys' fees should be mindful of a procedural mechanism known as an "offer of judgment." The purpose of the offer of judgment rule is to encourage settlements. Under the offer of judgment rule, if a written settlement offer *identified* as an offer of judgment is timely made by the school district at least two weeks before the hearing but is rejected by the parent and the final award following the hearing is *less* favorable than the offer of judgment that was made, this can greatly reduce or even eliminate the parent's opportunity to recover attorneys' fees and expenses.

Significantly, that result (winning less at hearing than what was offered in the offer of judgment) also exposes the recipient of the offer of judgment to being liable for the school district's "costs." These out-of-pocket expenses can be nominal but sometimes they can amount to thousands of dollars. In some jurisdictions, those costs may also include the school district's attorneys' fees. In most cases, the school district will *not* make an offer of judgment since doing so amounts to a capitulation. If a parent receives an offer of judgment, it is essential to consult with counsel before taking any action.[63]

The offer of judgment is a time-sensitive, double-edged sword. Some parents will want to take advantage of the certainty and relatively quick payment that an offer of judgment can provide. Others will take the risk of rejecting the offer of judgment, believing that they will do better at trial than the district's offer. The offer of judgment process is a little like the game of "chicken": This is not the time to overplay your hand.

The takeaway regarding offers of judgment is that when parents receive such an offer, they need to have a realistic discussion with their attorney to assess the likelihood that the parent will recover a sum *greater* than that specified in the offer of judgment. If, after that discussion, the parents and their attorney believe the issue is too close to call, parents should probably give serious consideration to accepting the offer of judgment.

How Should Parents Account for Insurance Benefits?

As a result of state-by-state insurance reform,[64] many more parents these days will have access to insurance benefits that, after satisfying any deductible or co-pay, will cover at least a *portion* of their programming expenses. There is no right to "double dipping"—parents may not be paid twice for the same service. Accordingly, those who are fortunate enough to receive insurance proceeds will need to disclose and account for them, either in the context of settlement discussions or at the hearing. This is not to say that if an insurance claim is denied that the parents are then obligated to exhaust the insurer's appeals process. Under those circumstances, it should be sufficient for the school district that there are no insurance proceeds to account for.

What happens if, after the school district settles and pays out the settlement

---

63 For example, assume for the moment that the parent's claim seeks reimbursement for a $100,000 school tuition plus the cost of the student's afterschool programming. Two weeks before the hearing, the school district makes an offer of judgment communicating that it will pay the $100,000 tuition, but not a penny for the afterschool programming. In that scenario, to "beat" the school district's offer of judgment, the parent would have to win the school tuition plus at least *some* money for the afterschool program. If the parent won only the tuition but nothing more, the offer of judgment rule would operate as to substantially preclude the recovery of attorneys' fees after the time that the offer of judgment was made.

64 While insurance reform had many supporters, a resounding thanks is due to Autism Speaks for aggressively garnering support for legislative action.

proceeds, the parent *later* receives insurance proceeds covering the same service? In that highly unusual situation, you will need to consult with counsel and probably your accountant as well.[65]

Gift or Loan—Which Makes the Most Sense?

Given the substantial costs associated with assembling a private program, if the opportunity presents itself, many families will turn to relatives or friends for financial assistance. Even those families with significant financial resources often find it difficult to sustain the cost of effective programming.

When parents bring a reimbursement case, the funds at issue need to be "at risk."[66] If the transaction is documented as a gift (e.g. a grandparent offers to pay the school tuition with no expectation of repayment), the school district may seek to dismiss the parent's reimbursement claim on the grounds that the parent has no standing to seek "reimbursement" recovery where the funds constituted a gift. For this reason, when parents obtain funds from a relative or friend, the transaction should be documented and recorded as a loan. This is true even if the loan is not interest-bearing.

Are Parents Ever Required to Pay the School District's Attorneys' Fees?

The fee-shifting provisions of the IDEA statute were designed to give prevailing parents the opportunity to recover attorneys' fees and costs. While such cases are extremely rare, some courts have directed parents to pay the school district's reasonable fees and costs where there is compelling evidence in the record demonstrating that the parents' case was frivolous and unfounded.[67]

---

[65] Parents who file itemized tax returns should also consult with their accountant to discuss the extent their therapy and related program expenses may be deductible and what income recapture may occur if out-of-pocket therapy expenses deducted for tax purposes in one year are later recovered from the school district. The acronym FAPE stands for a free and appropriate public education. Accordingly, while parents should always check with their accountant regarding the treatment of educational expenses and reimbursements, if a parent does not deduct any portion of their child's therapy expenses and the parent is later reimbursed for those expenses by the school district after raising a FAPE deprivation claim, that reimbursement is not supposed to represent income to the parent.

[66] The "at risk" rule in reimbursement cases brought under IDEA is similar to the rule any investor faces when purchasing shares of stock from an investment house. If the investor instructs his or her broker to invest $100 and the stock price jumps to $200 the next day, the investor is entitled to the $100 profit only if the investor actually *paid in* the $100 purchase price.

[67] In some jurisdictions, a parent who rejects the school district's offer of judgment may be required to pay the school district's attorney's fees if the parent does not win more relief than that specified in the offer of judgment.

If, for example, a parent files for a hearing against a school district claiming to be a resident of the school district, but it later comes out that the parent actually lives in an adjoining state (i.e. the filing was fraudulent), the parent could be ordered to pay the school district's attorneys' fees and costs.

No parent has ever been ordered to pay the school district's fees and costs simply because the parent lost and the school district won. Much more needs to be shown to hold a parent liable to pay for the school district's fees. Under the rule in question, a parent may be exposed to pay this kind of sanction if a judge finds the parents' claim to be "frivolous, unreasonable, and without foundation."

This potential threat is yet another good reason for parents to engage experienced, independent counsel. Attorneys are required to exercise independent professional judgment; they are not "hired guns." It is the attorney's job to investigate and review the record to make sure that any claims that are asserted are, in fact, meritorious and reasonably supported by the evidence. It is also the attorney's job to protect the parents, sometimes even from themselves. In all candor, if an attorney fails to do "due diligence" to make sure that the parents' claim was meritorious *before* filing, resulting in the parents being ordered to pay the school district's legal fees based on a finding that the parents had filed frivolous claims, those parents should probably consider suing their attorney for malpractice.

Chapter 9
Managing Safety Considerations

Parents of children on the spectrum know all too well that their children face special dangers that the neurotypical population will probably not experience. When, for example, you're standing at a busy street corner waiting to cross at the light, without even thinking about it, you're probably holding your child's hand a little bit tighter than the parent next to you. Okay, perhaps a lot tighter. Similarly, when your child is splashing around in a swimming pool, your body is on constant alert, ready to dive in to save the day. Parents respond subconsciously to many potential threats. There are, however, some risks and dangers that require active management and planning.

The "Elopement" Threat

When parents entrust their children to the care of the local school district, the expectation is that their children will be returned to them safe and sound. The scenario where this does not happen is every parent's nightmare. Elopement from school is one such threat—which becomes elevated if the student lacks a functional system of communication.

In 2014, non-verbal, 13-year-old New York City public school student Avonte Oquendo walked out of his school unchallenged by any teacher or security guard, never to be seen alive again. Avonte's disappearance galvanized the entire city. Months later, after literally thousands of volunteers had combed the city hoping for a miracle, Avonte's remains were found in the shallows of the East River. The entire city went into mourning.[68]

Given the constant local, national, and even international news coverage surrounding Avonte's disappearance, many New Yorkers assumed that the New York City Department

---

[68] Children with autism are often drawn to bodies of water regardless of whether they know how to swim. As soon as possible, parents should make sure their children are water-safe.

of Education and other school districts would implement new policies to make it next to impossible for a student to elope from school. Surely, New York's public schools had learned their lesson. Incredibly, however, in the year following Avonte's disappearance, there were a number of additional school elopements in the New York area. While, fortunately, none of these other situations resulted in tragedy, it was only due to dumb luck or the fortuitous intervention of a good Samaritan.

In one such case that my firm litigated, a New York City student with autism never made it onto his bus following school dismissal. Administrators saw this student leave the building and erroneously assumed that someone else was taking responsibility to get him onto his school bus. Unfortunately, however, no one did: the student walked off school grounds and spent the evening wandering the streets in subfreezing temperatures. He was still wandering the streets when he was spotted in the early morning hours by an alert police officer.[69]

Today, *Kevin and Avonte's Law*, a federal statute passed in 2018, funds training for law enforcement and schools to address the problem of wandering and school elopement. The New York City version of Avonte's Law, which I helped support, provides funding to ensure more school building entrances and exits will be alarmed. Most New Yorkers were surprised to learn that the exit door that Avonte used to elope was not alarmed. Even more surprising is that this failure apparently was systemic. How did New York City ever hope to keep its students in and the bad guys out without securing every school entrance and exit?

There are few anxieties greater than not knowing where your children are. Today, because of increased public awareness, the elopement threat has decreased somewhat—but it is impossible to ensure against human error. For greater peace of mind, some parents have invested in footwear, clothing, backpacks, watches, or bracelets containing GPS tracking devices. The market for "wearable" tracking devices has exploded in recent years, providing parents with many more options.[70]

Fire and Lockdown Drills

For students on the spectrum who may have difficulties with transitions—particularly those with sensory regulation challenges—there are few events more disturbing than a

---

[69] The police asked the student's parents to provide dental records to aid the search efforts. Given the subfreezing temperatures, they too apparently feared that the student might not make it through the night and that they might need those dental records to identify the student's body.

[70] While some parents might look down their nose at these kinds of devices as dehumanizing, relying on the protection of minimally invasive "wearables" is a far cry from permanently microchipping your child. I see wearables in the same category as life preservers that are worn temporarily for safety.

fire or lockdown drill. For some, these drills can be outright terrifying. While no statistics on this subject are available, it is my sense that few school systems take the time to pre-teach special needs students about the function of these drills, what they should expect, and the protocol for appropriate responses.

Failing to properly prepare (and desensitize) students for these drills can put students at risk for serious physical injury. One of our recent cases involving a high school student illustrates the dangers that can arise during drills that are "sprung" on vulnerable students without prior notice and preparation.

The case came to us after the fact. The student, "P.", was attending a self-contained, public-school classroom and had recently been assigned a new (male) aide. Without any advance notice, the student heard a walkie-talkie bark an announcement that his school was going into an immediate lockdown. Upon hearing this announcement, the classroom teacher told P. and her other students to turn off the lights, lock the door, pull down the blinds, and "hide."[71]

P. had watched other school shooting situations unfold on television, including Sandy Hook. No one explained to P. that the lockdown was "only a drill." P. believed that the lockdown was real and that there was an active shooter in the building. P. was afraid and went to hide in a closet with two other students.

Even after the lockdown drill was completed, no one told P. that the lockdown was only a practice drill or that it was safe for P. and the other two students to come out of the closet they had been hiding in. Apparently, P. and the two other students were not coming out of the closet fast enough for P.'s newly assigned aide. As P. testified, the new aide roughly yanked all three boys out of their hiding place one by one and threw them to the floor. The aide twisted P.'s leg and P. testified that he heard a "crack." P. was struggling to stand up. The aide sat on P.'s back and his legs in such a way that P. (who had asthma) protested that he could not breathe. The aide also grabbed P. roughly by his neck. The irony, of course, is that the purpose of a lockdown drill is to *protect* students from physical harm.

P. was escorted to see the school nurse, who did not provide any treatment. The school nurse did not even bother to examine P.'s leg, nor was he taken to the hospital for

---

[71] Today, active shooter trainings teach us that because so many mass shootings involve AR-15 type, high-capacity assault rifles, a locked door, while certainly better than nothing, actually offers little protection. The national average for first responders to appear on the scene is reported to be between 5–6 minutes. To buy some time, active shooter trainings recommend that a locked door be fortified with a barricade of desks, chairs, and the like. According to Corporal Christopher Mason of the Manchester, Vermont Police Department, when it comes to barricades intended to slow down an active shooter, "the bigger the better."

further assessment and treatment. The school's indifferent response was simply to call P.'s father and tell him that he needed to come to school to pick P. up because he was "out of control."

P.'s father picked him up from school and immediately brought him to see his regular pediatrician. At the recommendation of the pediatrician, P.'s father brought him to a local hospital where X-rays confirmed that P.'s right ankle was broken. The struggle between P. and the aide also injured P.'s elbow and his neck had visible "grab" marks from the aide's violent approach. Among the physical injuries that P.'s father photographed that day, there were also psychological consequences, with P. fearing to ever return to school.

School districts cannot assume that students understand the purpose of drills and what their responsibilities are when a drill is announced. Moreover, when drills are announced, it is imperative that students be made to understand that the drill is for practice. If the lockdown or fire threat is real, students need to be told that as well. Students on the spectrum need predictability and reliability. They also need to know that they can trust what they are being told by a teacher or administrator.

The COVID-19 Related Threat Of An Infectious School Environment

While there are no reported court decisions to illustrate this principle as at the time of printing, it is just a matter of time before some school system will be called to account for offering a student a classroom or other service that is set up in such a way that it fails to adhere to generally accepted standards and subjects the student to the unreasonable risk of virus transmission. Accent on the word "unreasonable." While the prudent school district must take reasonable precautionary measures, I think that it is safe to say that school districts will not be held responsible for eliminating all risk. I predict, however, that so long as we are under the cloud of an active pandemic, school districts will likely be held liable for failing to observe basic safety measures and standards, such as maintaining an appropriate social distance between students and not compressing students into unduly crowded classrooms that compromise what are deemed to be adequate social distance zones. For the time being, however, the current threat of another major outbreak occurring in the Summer or Fall of 2020 will likely mean at least another semester of virtual, largely remote instruction.

When Your Child is Coming Home (Or Going to School) with Unexplained Injuries

It is reasonable to expect a child with autism or a related disorder to come home from school with the occasional bruise—the same holds true for typically developing children. Minor bruises can and will occur during school hours. The scraped knee can simply be evidence of your child sliding into third base during recess.

There are, however, other kinds of bruises and marks that should be of legitimate concern to a parent, particularly for children with communication challenges who may not be able to explain "what happened." This includes any bruises or scrapes that you are seeing on a regular basis without any corresponding report from the teacher or some administrator. This also includes the kind of bruises often seen after a child has been physically restrained by a staff member.

When you see "grab" or pinch marks on your child's upper torso area or you can make out the outline of fingers, it is cause for alarm. Parents should document any unusual bruises or other marks by taking photos with a phone or other device with a time stamp. The next step is to request an immediate meeting with your child's teacher and the production of any "incident reports." If going to the teacher does not produce a satisfactory explanation, a parent has no choice but to contact the school principal or other administrator. Staff abuse or bullying by students may need to be ruled out. You also need to know if your child is being physically restrained for purposes of behavioral compliance. Ironically, physical restraint may be out of compliance and at odds with the express protocols of your child's behavior intervention plan or IEP mandates.

The equally problematic flipside of coming home with unexplained bruises is *arriving at* school with them. Teachers and other school personnel are "mandatory reporters" if there is any suspicion of child abuse. If your child is showing up at school with more than a small band-aid, you should email the teacher a brief "heads up" report as to what happened—if for no other reason than it might help explain any changes in your child's behaviors. If your child needs medical attention, get it. With increased public awareness of abuse, complaints can rest on a hair trigger. The last thing a parent needs is a phone call or knock at the door from an investigator from child protective services. If you do happen to get that phone call or knock at the door, you probably should contact counsel.

The Potential Danger of Police Encounters

Greater independence and self-sufficiency in the form of increased physical freedom in the community comes at a price. The greater the extent that individuals with autism are participating in the community, the greater the risk of a physical confrontation with police personnel. The risk of a physical confrontation is especially elevated in the highly combustible situation where the individual with autism is not ready, willing, or able to respond fast enough to questions or commands.[72] Police personnel can quickly up the

---

72 Individuals who are on the spectrum are considered especially vulnerable to trauma due to their

ante and become more aggressive if they conclude that the individual they are dealing with is "resisting" or treating them in a disrespectful manner.

Police regularly demand compliance from unfamiliar individuals. For individuals on the spectrum, compliance can be difficult even when the person directing compliance is known and trusted. These dynamics represent an ongoing problem for the autism community.

To protect the public, it is an entirely legitimate police function to be on the lookout for unusual behavior: the swerving driver who might be intoxicated, anyone seen sprinting out of a bank or department store, or the subway passenger who leaves their backpack on the seat of the train before exiting. It also is within normal police functioning to investigate situations that are called in to the police station.

When police officers spot and detain someone engaging in unusual behavior, they are trained to ask lots of questions—questions for which they expect immediate answers. "What is your name?" "Can I see some ID?" "Where do you live?" "Can I look in the trunk of your car?"

Police personnel often expect instantaneous compliance from citizens when they issue directives. "Put your hands where I can see them." "Step away from the car." "Put that phone down." "Stop walking away." "Lay face-down on the ground and put your hands behind your back." "Hey, I'm talking to you. Where do you think you're going?" We know that individuals with autism often have difficulties with transitions and processing: A police confrontation puts those concepts to the ultimate stress test.

When physical confrontations occur between the police and individuals who are on the spectrum, they can easily spiral out of control, sometimes with life-altering consequences. *People v. Reginald Latson*, a Virginia criminal matter, illustrates a serious potential threat that every parent should be aware of.

Reginald "Neli" Latson, a young African-American man first diagnosed at age 14 with Asperger's Syndrome, did not have many interests but loved spending time at his community library. Neli loved the quiet of the library and would often wait outside for the building to open. The library was Neli's refuge where he could spend hours; there was never a hint of a problem when he did so.

One day when Neli was waiting for the library to open, someone apparently called the local police precinct, saying there was a suspicious "man with a gun" standing

---

deficits in social communication and emotion regulation. See DW Hoover's 2015 article, "The Effects of Psychological Trauma on Children with Autism Spectrum Disorders," from the *Review Journal of Autism and Developmental Disorders*.

outside the library entrance. A police officer was dispatched to the scene to investigate.

When the officer arrived, he asked Neli some questions; apparently, there was no response. The police officer put his hands on Neli and directed him to lay face-down on the hood of his police cruiser. Between Neli's hypersensitive reaction to physical contact and his inability to respond instantaneously to the officer's commands, a dangerous wrestling match ensued. Somehow in the ensuing struggle, Neli forced the police officer to the ground, causing the officer to sustain some permanent paralyzing injuries when his head hit the pavement. Other police personnel then arrived at the scene and arrested Neli for assaulting a police officer and resisting arrest. As a result, what was supposed to be a quiet visit to the library turned into tragedy, with Neli facing criminal charges carrying up to a 10-year jail term.

There were two tragedies that day—the law enforcement officer was seriously injured while investigating a report of a suspicious "man with a gun." It was his job to ask Neli some questions and he did not know that Neli was not carrying a firearm. While we will never know for sure, many believe that the entire physical confrontation and resulting injuries could have been avoided had the police officer received meaningful training regarding individuals who may be on the autism spectrum.

Neli was tried and convicted of the most serious criminal charges; while he awaited sentencing, the local community in Virginia was clamoring for a very stiff sentence. It was not unthinkable that the sentencing judge would bow to public pressure and send Neli away for a long time. However, if Neli was sentenced to an extended prison term, he might not survive the experience; sentencing Neli to an extended prison term could easily amount to a death sentence.

Although Neli was represented by very able local criminal counsel, I was asked to advocate for him in my capacity at the time as the Director of the Autism Speaks Federal Legal Appeals Project. The following is the letter I sent to the sentencing judge, imploring him to consider the many mitigating factors.

AUTISM SPEAKS
It's time to listen.

May 18, 2011

Re: Reginald Latson

Dear Judge Sharp:

I am writing Your Honor in my capacity as the Director of the Autism Speaks[1] Federal Legal Appeals Project.[2]

Autism Speaks and its constituency have been following the *Latson* case with a great deal of concern. In the first instance, we have a great deal of concern and respect for the law enforcement officer who was seriously injured while doing his job in the line of duty. Our hearts go out to the officer and his family.

Rarely, if ever, does Autism Speaks advocate in connection with an active criminal matter. Autism Speaks, for example, will not involve itself in any matter where there is evidence that the defendant's "autism" is, in reality, a pretextual excuse that is "diagnosed" or "discovered" only *after* the arrest of the defendant. Those kind of defendants impair our cause, and serve only to confuse or offend the public. The defendant in *Latson*, however, has a longstanding autism diagnosis. Moreover, his behaviors are further impacted by his more particular diagnosis as having Asperger's Syndrome, also sometimes known as Asperger's Disorder. We urge that there are special circumstances here that warrant the exercise of this Court's sound discretion in processing and tempering the jury's sentencing recommendation.

We certainly do not fault the officer for investigating what he erroneously *believed* to be a suspicious man with a gun. In actuality, however, there was no gun, and the defendant was waiting for the library to open. Ironically, for Reginald, a young man with

---

[1] Autism Speaks is the world's largest not-for-profit organization dedicated to autism research, education and treatment. We have chapters across the United States, Canada and the United Kingdom, and work with federal, state, and local governments, as well as the U.S. military, to meet the treatment and educational needs of the ever-growing population of children diagnosed with autism.

[2] I also am writing as the founder of the very first law firm in the nation dedicated to the representation of students with autism spectrum disorders in matters arising under the federal Individuals With Disabilities Education Improvement Act, 20 U.S.C. Sec. 1415 et seq. In the last ten years, my law firm has represented nearly 700 students with autism (including dozens with Asperger's Syndrome) in more than 30 states. Some of the families we work with have one or more parents who are law enforcement officers, active state court judges, or in military service.

---

2 PARK AVENUE, 11TH FLOOR, NEW YORK, NY 10016 P: (212) 252-8584 F: (212) 252-8676

AUTISM SPEAKS
It's time to listen.

Asperger's Syndrome, the quiet library he was waiting to gain entrance to was serving as a place of refuge. We do not fault the officer for not knowing about Reginald's autism (Asperger's) disability, and how that core disability would be expected to impact and degrade (1) Reginald's ability to quickly process instructions and commands, (2) Reginald's ability to properly understand and "read" social cues and situations, and (3) Reginald's reaction to physical contact.[3] Unfortunately, however, between the officer's mistaken beliefs and perceptions and Reginald's erroneous social perceptions and his hypersensitive reaction to physical contact, a formula for disaster arose—a formula that then spiraled out of control to its inevitable conclusion. What happened here is every police officer's worst nightmare. For parents of children with autism, it is their worst nightmare as well.

For purposes of sentencing, we respectfully urge that Reginald's reactions and behaviors need to be understood as a manifestation of his autism disorder. It also must be kept in mind that Reginald's autism was first diagnosed at age 14, and that for this reason, intervention efforts addressing his autism started relatively late.

I know from personal experience with hundreds of families that students like Reginald can be systematically taught the communication and skills needed to *safely* navigate challenging situations. Behavioral intervention delivered and supervised by trained behavior analysts is a scientifically validated approach to effectuate that change, and those kinds of services are available within the scope of Reginald's school system.[4] They are not, however, available in any meaningful or effective form as part of further incarceration, and on this point, it is my understanding that Reginald has already been incarcerated for more than a year. Under the federal IDEIA statute and Virginia law, Reginald is entitled to intervention and teaching support (only) until he is 22.

If the purpose of sentencing is to punish Reginald and teach him a lesson, he already has been incarcerated for more than a year, and a longer incarceration will not likely have any greater impact to him as part of a teaching lesson. In fact, any further incarceration is likely to be counterproductive, and eliminate any chance that Reginald can be returned as a productive and functioning member of society. As Reginald is entitled to teaching and behavioral support from his school system only until age 22, that clock is ticking. The next few years of educational opportunity can be put to good use for

---

[3] In the last decade, "autism" training has become available for law enforcement and emergency first responders. Dennis Debbaudt, in particular, is a well known presenter who travels the country to provide such training. This training is designed to anticipate, neutralize and prevent autism-related situations from spiraling out of control.

[4] I am speaking of a professional at the level of a Board Certified Behavior Analyst, not merely a school psychologist or "counselor."

---

2 PARK AVENUE, 11TH FLOOR, NEW YORK, NY 10016 P: (212) 252-8584 F: (212) 252-8676

AUTISM SPEAKS
It's time to listen.

Reginald. Or, they can be frittered away. The law provides the opportunity for judicial review of the jury's sentencing recommendation. The legislature has thus presumed that there may be any number of reasons for the court to reject or significantly temper the sentencing recommendation of the jury.

Accordingly, for all the foregoing reasons, Autism Speaks is urging Your Honor to craft a sentence that will acknowledge Reginald's prior year of incarceration and direct immediate and appropriate behavioral treatment *and* ongoing maintenance of probation requirements to be directed by your Honor as an express condition of avoiding further incarceration time. This certainly is a serious case, but it also is one that requires a more careful and thoughtful analysis of the sentencing phase, taking into consideration the impact of Reginald's autism.

We thank Your Honor for giving Autism Speaks the opportunity to address the court.

Sincerely,

Gary S. Mayerson, Director
Autism Speaks Federal Appeals Project

2 PARK AVENUE, 11TH FLOOR, NEW YORK, NY 10016   P: (212) 252-8584   F: (212) 252-8676

Whether any credit is due to my letter or not, the sentencing judge rejected the prosecutor's recommendation for a 10-year jail term and, instead, sentenced Neli to a two-year term of imprisonment. Two years in prison obviously was a lot better than ten, but it was hardly cause for celebration. Neli was languishing in his jail cell. I worked closely with Bob and Suzanne Wright, the co-founders of Autism Speaks, to petition Governor Terry McAuliffe to exercise his discretionary clemency powers to assure Neli's transfer to a secure therapeutic facility in Florida—one that had been recommended by Virginia's mental health officials. Governor McAuliffe exercised his clemency powers, most likely saving Neli's life in the process.

Nick Pletnikoff's Traumatic Encounter with Police Personnel

On September 16, 2015, Nick Pletnikoff, then in his late twenties, walked out the front door of his Kodiak Island home to collect the day's mail—one of his regular chores. Nick knew his neighborhood well and was keenly aware of even the smallest changes in his physical environment. That day, Nick noticed there was an unfamiliar car parked in the special space reserved for one of Nick's neighbors. Nick saw that the car door was wide open and went to investigate.

It was not at all unusual for Nick to check out the cars in his immediate neighborhood. On occasion, Nick might lock a neighbor's car that he found unlocked. Nick was accepted as the neighborhood's self-appointed car monitor and parking attendant: Nick's neighbors accepted Nick's car-related quirks as entirely innocent. Everyone knew about Nick's quirks except, of course, the owner of the unfamiliar vehicle.

The owner of the unfamiliar vehicle, apparently visiting one of Nick's neighbors, was quite upset to see a young man (Nick) entering his car. He confronted Nick and told him to "take off." Unfortunately, while Nick would likely have responded to "Hey you, get out of my car!," Nick was not familiar with that particular idiomatic expression. Airplanes can "take off," but people? Nick was confused about what the visitor was asking him to do, so he remained on the scene, making the owner of the unfamiliar vehicle even more upset.

The owner of the unfamiliar vehicle told Nick that he was going to call the police—a warning that would send most people scurrying. Ironically, hearing that the police were being called was *reassuring* for Nick. Nick knew and liked a number of Kodiak Island police officers. Surely the police would know what to do! So, Nick continued to *remain* on the scene, waiting patiently for the police to come. When the owner of the vehicle asked Nick where he lived (a question Nick was familiar with), Nick dutifully gave the correct address.

As the police dispatch report indicates, the owner of the vehicle called police to complain that a young man had attempted to enter his vehicle and that the young man was still "standing there" even after he had told the young man to "take off." The owner of the vehicle communicated to the police dispatcher that the young man was "non-combative." The owner then offered that perhaps the young man was "high."

Minutes later, several police cruisers arrived. Nick was holding the mail from his family's mailbox and walking back to his home when an unfamiliar police officer wearing a bodycam approached Nick, grabbed him by the wrist and barked "Do you have any I.D.?" Nick, flustered, erroneously responded that he did not.[73]

When the officer commanded Nick to "put your hands behind your back," Nick did not immediately comply and was then forcibly bent over the trunk of a car. Nick can be heard and seen on the bodycam tape pleading over and over "I want to go home." There was then a further escalation of force with three adults now holding Nick on the ground and spraying pepper spray directly into Nick's eyes. In just seconds, the encounter between Nick and the Kodiak Island Police Department had gone from bad to worse to completely out of control.

Police bodycam photo of Nick Pletnikoff, 2015

One of the police officers on the scene knew Nick and also knew all about his autism, but inexplicably said nothing to the other responding officers. Had this informed police officer said something—anything—to the other responding officers, this disturbing encounter probably would never have happened.

---

73 Later, when another officer asked politely and calmly if Nick had any identification with him, Nick produced identification as well as a medical ID.

Dr. John McEachin, who had consulted with the Pletnikoff family at the time of the 1998 litigation with the Kodiak Island school system (see Chapter One), offered the opinion that Nick suffered serious physical and psychological trauma from the 2015 police confrontation—trauma that created intense feelings of helplessness and panic. Dr. Mulick, Nick's other consultant over the years, agreed.

Objective evidence showed that Nick had regressed after experiencing this trauma. He also had lost trust in figures of authority. There were other post-injury changes in his behavior, including increased sleeplessness, difficulty in following multi-step directions, loss of confidence, reduced impulse control, reduced independence, decreased concentration, and lowered frustration tolerance.

To address Nick's demonstrable regression, Dr. Mulick recommended desensitization and social skills therapies that included community travel, interaction with strangers, and interaction with people in uniform. Dr. Mulick also recommended that Nick have on his person a business card or medic-alert type wearable that would inform third parties that they were dealing with someone with special needs.[74]

Nick Pletnikoff boating, Summer 2019

---

[74] Reaching into a pocket to retrieve a business card during a police confrontation could easily pose grave dangers. A detainee reaching into a pocket or bag to pull out a business card might be shot by a police officer fearing that the detainee is going for a weapon. Because of this additional danger, wearing a medic-alert type bracelet is probably the safer alternative. When police question someone being detained and the detainee is not providing answers, police and other first responders need to be trained to ask themselves a simple question: "Does this person have a disability that makes it difficult or impossible for them to respond?"

The Pletnikoff family filed suit against the Kodiak Island Police Department and that case ultimately was settled. While the Pletnikoff family was able to put the lawsuit behind them, they still face a long road ahead. Nick continues to receive trauma therapy and cognitive behavior therapy to help him recover from his encounter with the police and the resulting global skill regression. The latest report is that Nick is making slow but steady progress.[75]

Managing the Threat of Food Allergies

Most school districts now recognize the life-threatening danger some students face due to allergies. Managing the threat of allergen exposure ensures safe access to the school environment. If you have a doctor's evaluation identifying known allergens, this is something that should be shared with the entire IEP team and incorporated prominently into the IEP so everyone involved with your child will be on the same page. This includes but is not limited to the school nurse.

Your IEP should contain a detailed action plan if your child is exposed to an allergen that can spark an anaphylactic (extreme, often life-threatening) reaction. That action plan should spell out whether or not an EpiPen or similar measure will be employed (and by whom) and provide for parents and the treating physician to be called immediately.

How to Manage Seizure Activity—The Seizure Action Plan

A significant percentage of the autism population will experience seizure activity by adulthood. This can range in severity from subclinical seizures to grand mal seizures. If your child has a history of seizure activity, it is imperative to share that with the school district for purposes of IEP development. If you are seeing a neurologist, you will want to share those recommendations with the IEP team.

Orrin Devinsky, MD, is the Director of the New York University Comprehensive Epilepsy Center in Manhattan and widely considered one of the world's leading neurologists and seizure specialists. According to Dr. Devinsky, "Epilepsy should not limit the vast majority of a child's activities and efforts for safe inclusion should be pursued, whether it is going on field trips to swimming. However, seizures can be extremely dangerous. The IEP should balance the needs for inclusion and participation with safety. A *seizure action plan* should be coordinated by the health care team and parents and communicated to the school to be adapted as needed to the setting and available personnel."

---

75 The Pletnikoff family, represented by local Kodiak counsel, brought a lawsuit for damages against the Kodiak Island Police Department. The case was settled for an undisclosed amount.

The seizure action plan that Dr. Devinsky refers to is a document detailing the school's response if the student should experience a seizure at school. It also identifies which individuals will be responsible to implement the plan. Essentially, the seizure action plan ensures that all concerned will be on the same page.

Managing Medications

Today, many students are taking medications under the care of a treating physician. In general, this is information that should be shared with the IEP team. This is especially true if the school nurse will have any responsibility to give or otherwise manage the medications or if the student needs to administer medications in a private setting or at a specified time that might conflict with class schedules.

When parents withhold information concerning medications, problems can arise. When, for example, a student has an adverse reaction to an adjustment in medication, it would be important for the teacher to be informed when the adjustment is implemented.

While parents should be mindful to share information about medications with the school district, the school district should exercise caution and restraint in presuming that a student needs to be taking a medication. It's one thing if the school district's physician member attends the IEP and recommends that a medication be considered. It is another thing when the classroom teacher makes a recommendation for medication because some other student did well with that medication. When a student is displaying inattention, sometimes the proper approach is a behavioral one and no medication is needed.

How Parents Should Respond to Evidence of Bullying

In 2007, our firm filed a demand for an IDEA-based hearing based on the core claim that one of our young clients, L.K., was being bullied in her third-grade classroom at PS 6, a public elementary school setting in Manhattan that had a reputation for academic excellence. We urged in our pleadings that the bullying abuse deprived L.K. of a FAPE. She was barely scraping by academically and the school attendance record showed one of the reasons why—L.K. was marked absent or late *forty-six* times during her most recent school year at PS 6.

We filed L.K.'s case years before states such as New York and New Jersey enacted anti-bullying legislation that, in most states, is now standard operating procedure. At the time, bullying was still being tolerated as some kind of inevitable rite of passage.

L.K. and her parents made several attempts to urge school administrators to address the bullying problem at PS 6. They tried to meet with the school principal, who refused to discuss the issue. L.K.'s parents made another attempt to discuss the bullying problem at L.K.'s annual IEP meeting but, once again, Ms. Fontana refused to allow any discussion about bullying. Essentially, the school's "see no evil, hear no evil" position was that there was no bullying at PS 6.

Today, many schools have a zero-tolerance policy towards bullying. In this case, absent a bona fide discussion, there was virtually no chance to address and alleviate the problem. At the end of their rope, L.K.'s parents did the only thing they could do to stop the bullying—they withdrew L.K. from PS 6 and placed her at the Summit School, a private, therapeutic school located in Queens.

By virtue of the Summit School being state-approved, New York City could have consented to the placement and had the State of New York pay the $30,000 tuition bill. Unfortunately, New York City decided to slog it out, denying there was any bullying going on at PS 6. New York City's fallback argument was that whatever may have happened to L.K. while at PS 6, it did not constitute a FAPE deprivation.

The hearing officer assigned to preside over the administrative hearing ruled that L.K. was a victim of bullying. The hearing officer also held that it was not reasonable for school authorities to claim that they were unaware of the bullying problem. However, at the end of the day, the hearing officer ruled that there was no FAPE deprivation because of her finding that L.K.'s educational opportunities were not significantly impaired by the bullying. The State Review Officer agreed.

On the parents' further appeal, the district court saw things a little differently. Judge Weinstein had held that "a disabled student is deprived of a FAPE when school personnel are deliberately indifferent to or fail to take reasonable steps to prevent bullying that substantially restricts a child with learning disabilities in her educational opportunities." Judge Weinstein addressed this issue and concluded that "if left unaddressed by the district," there was a "substantial probability" that bullying would severely restrict her educational opportunities during the next school year.

Judge Weinstein catalogued numerous red flags that revealed the "negative effects of bullying." These red flags included:

- ✓ L.K.'s almost daily complaints about being bullied at school
- ✓ L.K.'s emotional withdrawal and need to bring dolls to school
- ✓ The noticeable decline in L.K.'s happiness

- ✓ L.K.'s significant weight gain
- ✓ The manner in which L.K. had "shut down"
- ✓ L.K.'s growing lack of involvement
- ✓ How L.K. was ostracized in her classroom
- ✓ L.K.'s 46 incidents of being late or absent
- ✓ L.K.'s fear of going to school

Judge Weinstein held that procedurally, L.K.'s parents were deprived of the opportunity to participate meaningfully in the process of developing her IEP, by "effectively precluding all discussion of the critical issue of bullying." Substantively, Judge Weinstein ruled that L.K.'s IEP was deficient because it did not address the bullying problem L.K. was experiencing.

New York City refused to accept Judge Weinstein's decision and filed a further appeal with the Second Circuit Court of Appeals. The Court identified the salient issue to be decided: "We have not previously addressed whether the bullying of a student with a disability is an appropriate consideration in the development of an IEP and can result in the denial of a FAPE under the IDEA." The Court ultimately concluded that New York City "denied L.K. a FAPE by violating her parents' procedural right to participate in the development of her IEP."

Bullying Tips for Parents

Special needs students with IEPs are nearly four times as likely to be bullied than typically developing students. The L.K. case reveals a treasure trove of lessons for parents and school systems when dealing with a bullying situation.

- Don't wait for a bullying situation to resolve itself over time—early intervention is key
- Watch for bullying warning signs (visible injuries, changes in your child's emotional state, significant weight changes, excessive lateness or absences, withdrawal from friends, property destruction, etc.)
- Investigate the situation quickly. Ask your child questions and take photos
- Let your child know that you are proud of them for informing you and that it's not their fault
- Speak with your child's teachers and providers
- Make an appointment to speak with the school principal
- Request "incident reports"

- Call for an emergency IEP meeting
- Consider an anti-bullying plan within the IEP
- Only the bully should be punished (e.g. move the bully to another location, not the victim)

For more bullying tips for parents, see Appendix E (page 211) for a Q&A with Michael Dreiblatt of the not-for-profit STAND UP to Bullying.

How Parents Should Respond to Evidence of Sexual Abuse

When a school district fails to fulfill a service mandated by the student's IEP, the student can be made relatively whole by an award of compensatory education. Nothing, however, can ever fully remedy the long-term trauma and related damage that results from sexual abuse. Victims of sexual abuse often will report residual, PTSD[76] effects many years after the incident itself. Sexual abuse is not the claim you ever want to try and "win"—rather, it is the claim you want to *prevent* from ever arising.

As horrendous as sexual abuse is in every circumstance, it is most despicable when the victim is a child with a developmental disability and the perpetrator is a teacher, coach, or other individual entrusted to protect children. While defendants in sex abuse cases often seek to justify their conduct on the grounds that the sexual conduct was "consensual," courts uniformly agree that no consent can be given where the victim is a child with a developmental disability.

According to data recently retrieved for National Public Radio by the Justice Department, a student with a developmental disability is *seven times* more likely to be sexually abused than typical peers. Fully 40% of sexual assaults will take place during the day, with some of these criminal incidents taking place at school. These crimes "go mostly unrecognized, unprosecuted and unpunished, with the abuser free to abuse again" ("The Sexual Assault Epidemic No One Talks About," *All Things Considered*, January 8, 2018). Given the overwhelming evidence uncovered in connection with the Bill Cosby, Penn State, and church scandals, this state of affairs should come as no surprise. No parent or school can take the position that "it can't happen here." Today we know better. Sexual abuse can happen anywhere, and it does.

Sexual abuse perpetrators often "target" and "groom" their victims. Students with developmental disabilities, especially those with communication challenges, are selected as victims precisely because they are less likely to "tell" and are more easily manipulated and intimidated. And if they do ever tell, their words are less likely to be

---

76 Post-Traumatic Stress Disorder.

believed. Students with autism and other disabilities may be seen by perpetrators as the perfect victim.

Lessons Learned from Doe v. Darien

A few years ago, I received a call from the parents of an elementary school student ("John")[77]. With the support of a one-to-one paraprofessional, John had been attending a public elementary school in Darien, Connecticut.

John, using age-appropriate language for a twelve-year-old, had revealed to his parents, school personnel, his therapist, police investigators, and members of the Lower Fairfield County Sexual Assault Response Team (SART) that he had been sexually abused by his paraprofessional, Zachary Hasak. John had never before leveled such a charge against anyone and there were no witnesses to the alleged abuse.

Hasak, John's paraprofessional, never finished college but he was well-connected in the local community. His uncle had served as the mayor of one of the largest cities in Connecticut, his brother was a physician, his mother was a nurse, and (at the time he was hired to serve as John's one-to-one paraprofessional) his aunt, Robin Pavia, was the town of Darien's director of special education services. Somehow, Hasak managed to be hired for this important role without having *any* prior paraprofessional experience.

After John's parents met with Darien's administrators to discuss the shocking information John had revealed to them that morning over breakfast, Hasak was called into Darien's administrative offices and told by a supervisor of the serious charges that had been leveled against him. Given what was at stake, if ever there was a time for Hasak to utter the words "It's not true" or "I didn't do it," this was the time to do so. Significantly, however, Hasak did not deny any of the charges. Hasak said nothing—not a word. Hasak's sole response was to quietly weep. He then left the building (without denying any of the charges).

To the frustration of John's parents, the local prosecutor declined to file any criminal charges against Hasak. With no eyewitnesses and with John unlikely to be able to face down Hasak in Court, it would have been extremely difficult to prove beyond a reasonable doubt that Hasak sexually abused John. The local prosecutor, apparently weighing the odds, decided not to present any criminal charges against Hasak. Accordingly, John's family's only hope of getting any measure of justice was via a civil rights action in federal court.

---

[77] At the family's request, the actual identity of "John" and his parents was protected in the lawsuit by using court-approved assumed names.

Despite the many anticipated challenges and hurdles, we took the case to trial because of its importance to the family and the entire special needs community. Darien and Hasak were contending that John lacked the mental capacity to understand and tell the truth about being sexually abused. If that dangerous principle were ever accepted, perpetrators would be able to sexually abuse students with impunity. As John's father put it, it would be "open season" on people with disabilities. We considered it essential to establish the principle that people with developmental disabilities have the fundamental right to be heard and believed just like people without developmental disabilities. A lot was at stake.

We survived motion after motion and ultimately, after jury selection, the trial was scheduled to start in New Haven Connecticut in the blistering heat of summer 2015.

John's account of the alleged abuse had been videotaped as part of the SART team's investigation. Over the objections of the defendants, United States District Court Judge Janet Arterton admitted the videotape of John's interview into evidence so that it could be considered by the jury. The jury thus had the opportunity to see and hear John's actual words and demeanor at or about the time he complained about Hasak's alleged abuse. John's account on the videotape was both compelling and disturbing.

The jury also heard from John's treating psychiatrist, Dr. Gallo, and had the opportunity to see Dr. Gallo's treatment notes after they were received in evidence. Dr. Gallo had multiple consulting contracts with Darien for other students—contracts Darien was not required to renew. How many of those contracts would be renewed after Dr. Gallo testified on John's behalf? Dr. Gallo, a critical witness, had nothing to gain and everything to lose by testifying. I was never prouder of a witness than when Dr. Gallo took to the witness box and swore to tell the truth, the whole truth, and nothing but the truth.

Dr. Gallo's therapy treatment notes were especially compelling, as John explained in his own words what Hasak did and where and when he did it. Through Dr. Gallo's treatment notes, the jury heard John's account of Hasak allegedly rubbing himself on John and "glue" coming out. Dr. Gallo testified that from the perspective of an innocent, 12-year-old prepubescent boy, John's "glue" reference was a reference to Hasak ejaculating semen.

Dr. Gallo's treatment notes also referred to Hasak threatening John and his family. Dr. Gallo explained that it is not at all unusual for sexual predators to threaten victims and their families. They engage in such conduct to intimidate their victims into silence. [78]

The defendants' attorneys tried every possible tactic to discredit Dr. Gallo. Darien's Harvard-educated expert witness, Dr. Clark, received about $30,000 to attack the testimony and findings of Dr. Gallo. Strangely, besides attacking Dr. Gallo, Dr. Clark was not asked to go any further. Dr. Clark admitted that he was not hired to investigate and determine whether or not John had been sexually abused by Hasak.

Dr. Clark testified on direct that he was a "board-certified forensic psychiatrist;" however, he admitted during cross-examination that he had allowed his board certifications to lapse, he was not subject to the ethics rules that govern the conduct of physicians, he had observed John for no more than 45 minutes, and he had relatively little experience with John's particular disability. From my perspective, I thought that Dr. Clark came off as the quintessential "hired gun." I hoped that the jury would agree.

The school district's other witnesses testified that for instructional and behavioral management purposes, Hasak was repeatedly permitted to take John into an empty L-shaped classroom and that John and Hasak might have been left alone for up to 20 minutes at a time. Hasak's time with John was largely documented in "data sheets," but there were gaps of time that were not accounted for. The evidence established that Hasak had the *opportunity* to abuse John in a relatively private setting.

Virtually every day of the trial, Hasak came with an entourage that included an attractive young woman sitting by his side. Ostensibly, Hasak's intended message to the jury was "How can I possibly be guilty of sexually abusing a young boy when I'm obviously attracted to women?" We hoped that the jury would be sophisticated enough not to take this bait any more than the jury in Bill Cosby's criminal case bought the argument that Cosby did not need to drug women to "make" them have sex with him because he was, well, Bill Cosby. In our case, the jury did not have to decide *why* Hasak allegedly abused John sexually—only whether he had engaged in the alleged conduct.

When Hasak took the witness stand during the trial, he was not the same Hasak who had earlier wept and failed to deny the charges. This time, Hasak coolly and categorically denied that he ever abused John. In point of fact, this new and improved Hasak had an answer for everything. While other Darien witnesses admitted that Hasak and John were left alone in the empty classroom for up to 20 minutes, Hasak claimed that he was alone with John for no more than five minutes. He waved off all the disturbing entries in Dr.

---

78 "When Is Speech Violence?", an article by Lisa Feldman Barrett from the *New York Times* (7/16/17), asks the question, "Which is more harmful, the punch or the threat?" Barrett also writes that "Words can have a powerful effect on your nervous system." In the case against John's paraprofessional, both types of harm were at issue.

Gallo's treatment notes as if they were nothing.

At least a few jaws dropped in the courtroom when, during cross-examination, I forced Hasak to admit that he had an acting role in the hit film *Stepmom* (costarring Julia Roberts, Susan Sarandon, and Ed Harris). We had discovered this evidentiary gift during a routine Google search of Hasak's name. Actors make their living pretending to be someone else; we hoped the jury would conclude that this was precisely why Hasak was able to remain so calm and collected on the witness stand.

From the start, the defendants' core strategy to silence John and his accusations was to portray him as too disabled to tell the truth, but smart enough to make it all up. The defendants also suggested that John was "highly suggestible" and had been coached by his parents. And that perhaps John had a "bad dream" or was merely "scripting" from a show he may have seen on television. As a last-ditch effort, the defendants claimed that the videotaped interview of John conducted by the Lower Fairfield County Sexual Assault Response Team was "tainted." The Darien school district had *participated* in that videotaped interview, so the defendants' "tainted" argument simply didn't hold water. Over defendants' objection, Judge Arterton allowed the jury to see and hear the videotape evidence. The videotape was critical, given that John did not testify at the trial.

During my summation to the jury, one thing I focused on was Hasak's claim that he was left alone with John for no more than five minutes. Aside from the fact that others had testified that Hasak had up to twenty minutes of "alone" time with John, the suggestion was that five minutes is not enough time for an act of sexual abuse to occur. Really? I told the jury that an act of sexual abuse can happen in less than *one* minute. To drill down on that important point, for exactly one minute, I repeatedly took off my suit jacket and put it back on as many times as I was able. Just as a picture paints a thousand words, a simple demonstration can be very effective.[79]

During summations, the defendants challenged the jury with the theme "Why should we believe John's words?" My response was "Why *shouldn't* we? Because if you do not, you will send the worst kind of message that the words of a person with a disability mean and are worth less than the words of the rest of us."

After being given a series of instructions and written questions, the jury retired for deliberations. At defendants' insistence, the very first written question the jury was

---

[79] Courtroom demonstrations can also be disastrous when the unexpected occurs. A good example of a courtroom demonstration gone terribly wrong is O.J. Simpson being asked by prosecutors to put on the weathered glove that, by all appearances, did not fit. That demonstration gone wrong prompted attorney Johnnie Cochran's memorable closing admonition "If the glove doesn't fit, you must acquit."

required to answer was whether or not Hasak sexually abused John. The jury deliberated for two days, intermittently sending written questions to the court or asking for selected evidence to be revisited. One of the jury's questions was whether Hasak's name would ever appear on a sex offender registry. Unfortunately, as this was a civil and not a criminal matter, that would never happen. On the other hand, if Hasak was found liable for sexual abuse, that fact would likely appear indefinitely during a routine Google search of Hasak's name.

Waiting for the jury's verdict was excruciating, especially for John's parents. We could speculate, but ultimately everything was in the hands of the jury. We were with John's family across the street at a coffee shop when we received a text message from the court clerk that the jury had concluded its deliberations and that all counsel should return to the courtroom immediately.

When we returned to the courtroom, we watched intently as the jurors filed in and took their usual seats. Nothing in the jurors' expressions telegraphed what their verdict might be. I looked behind me. Hasak and his entourage also was looking for any sign of a verdict, but there was none. I knew that whatever was the jury's verdict, we had done our very best. We had spared no effort attempting to secure justice for John.

Judge Arterton asked the foreman whether the jury had reached a verdict. The foreman said "yes." The Court then directed its attention to the jury's first question. All of our efforts hung on a one-word response, "yes" or "no."

The foreman reported to Judge Arterton that the jury's answer was "yes": they had found that Hasak had sexually abused John. While the foreman's report meant we had won the trial, I can't say that I was elated. After all, the jury's verdict necessarily confirmed the horrendous wrong that had been done to victimize this young man.

I was, however, grateful that John had been validated as a human being—his words were believed, despite his obvious challenges. His parents' efforts were also vindicated. This time it was Hasak who was silenced. No appeal was filed. For my part, the jury's evident respect for John's words was worth far more than the dollar value of the substantial damages and attorneys' fees awarded by the Court. To date, considering the significance of the jury's verdict, this case remains the single most important case I've ever tried.

Doe v. Darien illuminates some simple measures that parents and school districts can take to minimize the opportunity for acts of sexual abuse to occur, or to continue undiscovered.

✓ In general, other than possibly "pull out" speech therapy and the like, no student should ever be left alone with a single adult behind closed doors—there is built-in safety and accountability when other adults are present or at least in the immediate vicinity.

- ✓ No student should ever be taken to an empty classroom or to a room with concealed sections that cannot be seen from the entrance door. Abuse is more likely to occur if a would-be perpetrator acquires an expectation of privacy—one good reason why supervisors should regularly make unannounced appearances throughout the school building.
- ✓ All instructional/therapy/behavioral support time should be documented and accounted for and those records should be regularly reviewed by supervisory personnel.
- ✓ Nobody is above the law. Hasak was the nephew of Darien's Special Education Director. There was evidence that when John spoke to his classroom teacher about Hasak, the teacher's response was to tell John to stop saying such things, because continuing to do so might get Hasak "in trouble."
- ✓ It's a serious red flag when students show or express fear concerning a school employee.

Finally, if a student tells a trusted adult about being sexually abused, that complaint should be immediately brought to the attention of all concerned: supervisors, the child's parents, child protective services, and the police. Waiting too long to contact the police can impair evidence gathering and endanger any potential criminal proceedings.

Chapter 10
Dealing with Suspensions and Other Disciplinary Proceedings

More students on the autism spectrum have the opportunity to be educated in less restrictive settings than ever before. While this trend is good news for promoting increased independence and self-sufficiency, it necessarily comes with higher expectations from teachers and administrators. The expectation is that students on the spectrum must conform to, or closely approximate, the behavioral norms associated with the neurotypical population. As unrealistic and inappropriate as it might be, some teachers and administrators following a "disciplinary" model may seek to enforce those expectations even for students who are attending self-contained, special education classrooms.

Many schools follow a published code of conduct that enumerates prohibited behaviors for which there ostensibly is "zero tolerance." Too many school administrators rush to invoke these rules of conduct to suspend or even expel students before implementing other strategies to address the fact that the root cause of the offending behavior may be a manifestation of the student's diagnosis. Or, they may call an IEP meeting to discuss a convenient remedy they say would be "best" for the student: moving the offender into a more restrictive classroom and program.

When school districts rush to judgment and take such steps, they can violate the IDEA statute's "least restrictive environment" mandate. As discussed in Chapter 4 (page 43), that mandate directs school districts to support students in less restrictive settings even if doing so requires additional aids and supports. Translation: School districts may be required to employ additional measures before taking action to move a student into a more restrictive setting.

Assume, for example, that a student attending an inclusion classroom is prone to overreacting to provocations from other students. The student reacts to an insult by overturning the other student's desk. After overturning the other student's desk for the second time, the offender is suspended for five days.

In an ideal world, no student should ever overturn another student's desk. But what steps did the school district take to manage and mitigate the offending student's behaviors? What, if anything, was done to secure the student's ongoing attendance and success? Was the student offered counseling or social skills training? Was a behavior analyst called in to assist and support the situation? Was a behavior plan ever developed? What, if anything, was done about the other student who arguably provoked the behavior? Was the offending student considered for a 1:1 aide? Under the IDEA statute, these considerations are supposed to be on the school system's due diligence menu.

Moreover, when suspensions reach a certain level, the school system may be required to convene a "manifestation" hearing where the core inquiry is whether the student's offending behavior was caused by the student's disability. If the offending behavior is deemed to have "manifested" itself because of the student's disability, the student may be entitled to special protections and accommodations that would be denied to a neurotypical student.

The Zero-Tolerance Policy that Went Too Far

School principals have a great deal of punitive power at their disposal. Some years ago, the parents of a thirteen-year-old girl attending a public school program engaged my firm to help them navigate a "principal's hearing" that would decide whether the student was going to be expelled from school for having a "knife" in her backpack.

The school had a published "zero-tolerance" policy regarding all potential weapons, so despite the diminutive size of the student's knife (a miniature pen knife about the size of a small nail clipper), the school principal had the power to do pretty much what he wanted.

The record we made revealed a number of mitigating factors. The student's father had recently been hospitalized and the student had recently been mugged. The student was feeling very vulnerable. Keeping the miniature pen knife at the bottom of her backpack was comforting and made her *feel* more confident. The student never once pulled out or opened the pen knife. She had never been in any trouble and had just celebrated her Bat Mitzvah. She was hardly a danger to anyone. The only reason the pen knife became an issue was because the student's former friend told the school's administrators that her "friend" was violating school policy by having the pen knife in her backpack.

Based on the school's "zero-tolerance" policy against students possessing any weapons, the school principal's knee-jerk position was that the student should simply be expelled. In other words, the principal's position was that the student should be punished as severely as if she had come to school brandishing a gun.

Fortunately, the presiding hearing officer did not share the principal's view of what would be an appropriate punishment. The hearing officer had the good judgment and wisdom to impose a meaningful consequence that the student would not soon forget, but one that was not so serious as to interfere with the student's plans to attend college.

Inappropriate Physical Contact

People with developmental disabilities have the same drives and interests as the neurotypical population. However, they may not have the same capacity to *regulate* their thoughts and urges so that their behavior conforms to societal expectations.

Some years ago, we received a call from the family of a male high-school student diagnosed with Asperger's who had just been suspended for touching a female student's breasts over her blouse. The female student involved had not lodged a complaint. In this case, an administrator walking the halls observed the touching firsthand, which set the suspension in motion.

The male student explained to us that he had asked the female student if he could touch her breasts, and she said "yes." When we investigated further, we learned that the female student had, in fact, given her consent to be touched because she "felt sorry" for the male student. There apparently was another female student who had allowed the male student such liberties for the same reason. In essence, the two girls had agreed to be felt up in the school hallway on a "mercy" basis.

The above situation could easily have been prevented by social skills training or counseling, reinforcing that there is a right time and place for everything. I give credit to the male student for at least seeking consent; however, he had to learn that even with consent, there are some things that you are not supposed to do in a high-school hallway.

Plagiarism and Other Acts of Academic Dishonesty

My sense is that far too many students on the autism spectrum fail to appreciate the nuances between plagiarism and defensible "research." In the "cutting and pasting" rush to complete and turn in a paper on time, they may forget to use quotation marks or give appropriate attribution, creating the erroneous impression that all the words and thoughts expressed are their own. Teachers and administrators might assume all students "should" understand how to give proper attribution, but this simply is not the case—any more than assuming that all students on the spectrum can properly apply *The Elements of Style* (Strunk & White) or have the social skills to navigate the many interpersonal challenges they may face.

It is not enough to have a rule against plagiarism for a population that often has difficulties with auditory processing and reading comprehension. Students on the spectrum need to be taught explicitly what plagiarism is and how to give attribution credit to sources. The student then needs to affirmatively demonstrate that they understand what plagiarism is and the adverse consequences of presenting another person's writing as your own. If you intend to hold a student to a relatively complex standard of behavior, it is imperative to teach that standard.

If there was a way to "profile" the kind of students who cheat on exams in a concerted, concealed, and premeditated manner, the neurotypical student population would win that contest hands down.[80] It take special skills to plan and execute premeditated cheating—"skills" that students on the spectrum often lack. This is not to say that students on the autism spectrum never get caught cheating on exams. It happens. However, when they are caught cheating, the cheating often is in plain sight, with the clumsy "cheater" oblivious to being observed and to the consequences of getting caught.[81]

In recent years, one of our clients was caught cheating on a physics exam in high school. She had repeatedly looked at her iPad to remind herself of a rule needed to complete the exam. The student did so *multiple* times right in front of the test proctor. All electronic devices had been specifically banned from the test site so, in this instance, the cheating violation was pretty obvious. When confronted, the student admitted that she glanced at her iPad several times during the test because she could not visualize and recall the rule; she had "panicked."

While the student admittedly had cheated in a state of panic and violated the school's rule against electronic devices during exams, it's clear there was no

---

[80] Those in doubt need only Google "high school cheating scandals" or the recent national college cheating scandal involving celebrities and coaches. Sadly, cheating to increase the chances of getting into a competitive college has become rampant. It is so widespread that parents have gotten into the act, serving prison sentences and paying fines for fraudulent and deceptive conduct.

[81] A good example of this phenomenon is the scene in the film *One Flew Over the Cuckoo's Nest* where characters played by Jack Nicholson, Danny DeVito, and others are playing a game of cards. Jack Nicholson challenges Danny DeVito's play by turning to him and asking loudly "Martini, are you cheating?" DeVito, still staring down at his cards, responds innocently "Yes" and continues playing as if he has done nothing wrong.

premeditated *plan* to cheat on the physics exam. This student had to have been the worst cheater ever. Really, what test taker would look at their iPad repeatedly right in front of a proctor? This student's naivete probably saved her from being expelled.

Chapter 11
The Threat of Criminal Charges

When individuals with autism are arrested, very often the arrested individual does not understand that what they were doing was wrong in the eyes of the law. While there is a general principle that "ignorance of the law is no excuse," most prosecutors understand that when individuals with autism violate the law, they normally have no intent to do so. The risk of arrest is part of the "cost" of including individuals with autism in our communities. The unthinkable alternative is to exclude individuals with autism from society.

Indecent Exposure Situations

Last summer, I received a telephone call from a parent who had just returned from the Jersey shore. Her son, eighteen years old and a full-grown young man, apparently accumulated a great deal of sand in his bathing suit—sand that was irritating him to no end. He acted decisively, pulling off his bathing suit and then shaking out the sand in front of scores of beachgoers, many of whom were families with young children. He was promptly arrested and ticketed for indecent exposure by police personnel who did not appreciate that there were mitigating factors. The charges were ultimately dropped.

The Potential Danger of Accessing Child Pornography

For many individuals on the autism spectrum, the internet represents a relatively safe zone where they can relax, kick back, and communicate in private without being threatened or judged. The problem is that there are other individuals operating in this ostensibly safe venue who have a different agenda. There are police detectives who troll the internet hoping to identify, entrap, and prosecute individuals who are producing, accessing, or watching child pornography.

Please understand, I am not defending the dehumanizing scourge of child pornography. It's a serious crime. However, it is all too easy for young, naive adults with autism to get themselves in trouble with this kind of internet content. Individuals with autism may see sexuality depicted on Netflix and other mainstream media.[82] They may assume that if graphic content is appearing on their computer screen, it must be okay—and may not appreciate when the "lines" begin to blur and cross into criminal territory.

Take, for example, a young adult with Asperger's in the basement of his parents' home, looking for interesting content on the internet. That young adult may not suspect that anything is awry when he receives the message "Hey, would you like to see naked pics of a thirteen-year-old girl?" He might not even appreciate his own adult status when opening the content. That naïve exchange might be followed up shortly by a knock at the door and a police cruiser parked at the curb.

While a police visit of this kind may not result in a full-blown arrest, prosecution, and conviction, this kind of trouble is largely avoidable. Parents have the responsibility to have frank, direct discussions about staying away from the kinds of sites and online inquiries that can result in serious legal problems—no matter how uncomfortable these conversations might be. There also are blocks and restrictions that can be put in place to limit access to the internet.

---

82 The sexuality deemed acceptable in today's mainstream media might have given rise to criminal proceedings just a few decades ago.

Chapter 12
When a Residential Placement May Be Warranted

Over the years, a few cynical school district administrators have communicated to me their belief that some parents are looking for any excuse to "get rid" of their child by placing them in a residential setting. My experience with families over more than two decades is definitely to the contrary. Residential placement can mean sending a child hundreds of miles from home. Unless residential placement has become the only realistic option, most families we work with are prepared to do anything to keep everyone under the same roof. And when the options point to a residential setting, families tend to look for programs that are close enough to reach by car.

There is nothing written in stone to signal when it is appropriate for parents to consider a residential program. But there are a number of factors that would point in favor of considering a residential placement. According to Vincent (Vinnie) Strully, the founder and CEO of the renowned New England Center for Children ("NECC"):

"In general, each child impacted by autism and related disorders is a unique case. It is impractical to apply a one-size-fits-all rule when it comes to pursuing a residential placement. The decision should be made in close collaboration with all stakeholders, including (but not limited to) the family, school district, and the appropriate clinicians and specialists. Open and honest communication about the child's successes and obstacles is imperative, assessing both the home and school environments. When weighing the decision to pursue residential treatment, consider the following:

1. Stakeholders need to be working collaboratively to improve the life of the child, which includes identifying individual or program limitations. What are the current needs of the child due to the severity or complexity of his/her disability? Is the current program able to address those needs or is there potentially a modification of the program or environment needed?

2. How does the home situation look? Is the family able to function and is the child gaining independence with activities of daily living? Independence in daily activities is imperative to future success and must be part of the child's program. Is additional support needed within the home environment? Are home-based services in place? Is a more collaborative approach needed between the child's school and home-based services? Is the child making sustained progress both in the presence and absence of service providers within the home environment?

3. Is the child at a point where remaining in the current situation is detrimental to his/her future success? Parents, school districts, and other stakeholders need to use a collaborative, informed approach to this decision-making process. Special consideration should also be made to the emotional and mental toll this decision could have on all members of the family.

4. Additionally, if it is deemed appropriate to seek out a residential placement, the team must consider the quality of the programs they are considering. A quality residential program is one with 24/7 comprehensive, consistent care utilizing appropriate teaching and clinical methodology to fit the needs of the individual child. Unfortunately, such high-quality programs may be difficult to find."

Once the decision is made to consider residential programs, Strully has identified the principal factors parents and professionals should consider in assessing the appropriateness of a program:

- Are there appropriate peers?
- Are there safety protocols in place?
- Is staffing appropriate and adequate for your child?
- How are weekends and evenings covered?
- Administration and Board of Directors oversight
- Methodology (e.g. ABA)—do you trust it and are you on board?
- Are the program facilities well-maintained?
- Is the educational instruction high-quality?
- Is there outcome data?
- Are there enrichment activities available (art, music, leisure)?
- Comprehensive approach (all services work together on behalf of the child)
- What medical services are available?
- What is the level of community access?

- How are the parents involved (staying connected to the child and school)?
- What are the staff's credentials?
- What is the program's expertise and reputation?
- Does the program offer vocational preparation and support?

There are not nearly enough quality residential programs to serve the autism community and the better programs have long waiting lists. In addition, programs in high demand have less incentive to accept a student who is about to age out of the public education system. For this reason, if your child, at 15, already needs to be placed in a residential program, it may be more prudent to secure the residential program at that time instead of waiting until the child turns 18 or 19. Also, when the student transitions to adulthood, it may be easier to implement a transition to an adult placement if that student already has been placed residentially.

Chapter 13
Preparing For the Transition To Adulthood—
The Main Event

When it is again safe to go out for a nice dinner, if you happen to be a dessert kind of person, you know that there are some classic dessert choices usually available at the end of the meal. New York cheesecake, key lime pie, and seven-layer cake fall into that category. If, however, you are partial to Chocolate Soufflé, you know that this is an altogether different process requiring some early intervention–style decision-making. After menus are circulated, your server will probably alert you that if you're thinking about ordering the chocolate soufflé, you'll need to place your order right away so that the kitchen will have it ready when it's dessert time.

Like chocolate soufflé, the transition to adulthood is not a fast-food recipe. The transition process will not be the equivalent of a light switch you flick on or off. It's supposed to be a well-coordinated, step-by-step process that takes place over time in multiple venues. Transition, much like a chocolate soufflé, turns out best when preparation begins early.

So, what exactly is transition planning? In theory, it's creating a coordinated set of activities to assist the development of skills, strengths, and preferences in the areas of:

- ✓ Employment and vocational skills
- ✓ Post-secondary education
- ✓ Community involvement
- ✓ Independent living
- ✓ Advocacy and self-determination

Looking at the above activities, there is no question but that the COVID-19 pandemic has had an adverse impact on students interested in pursuing transition entitlements directed to vocational training, community involvement and opportunities and other post-secondary goals. To say the least. An adverse impact is all but guaranteed when almost overnight, the nation's schools, colleges and universities are ordered closed along with restaurants, retail outlets and corporate offices, and where tens of millions of individuals lose their jobs and livelihoods.

There is, however, one very useful and valuable consequence of the pandemic that will likely help to enhance and accelerate transition assessments and vocational sampling. I am speaking of Zoom and the other forms of telehealth "remote" teaching technology that so many people learned to adapt to when the pandemic arrived, forcing millions to work remotely from home. This technology makes the assessment procedure so much easier to accomplish and it is now possible to *record* the entire assessment so that there are no lingering questions. This technology also obviates the need to travel to sample vocational activities that may be of interest. The technology is easily adaptable for a number of transition-related applications including:

- ✓ Vocational assessments
- ✓ Vocation sampling
- ✓ Parent training
- ✓ Job training
- ✓ Check-ins for individuals living on their own
- ✓ Supervision
- ✓ Counseling
- ✓ Probing for generalization and independence
- ✓ Staff meetings
- ✓ Eligibility interviews
- ✓ Behavioral and other consultation
- ✓ Development of goals and objectives
- ✓ Convening IEP and other meetings

Most importantly, with the pandemic still an active threat, remote teaching technology is continuing to save lives. As of May, 2020, CUNY Law School and other schools within the City University system in New York, for example, have already planned that the Fall, 2020 semester will continue to be taught virtually. Many, if not most other schools will likely do the same.

Transition planning under the federal IDEA statute is something that should start *years* before a student is scheduled to exit the public-school system. It is not a process that is supposed to take place when your student is ordering his or her cap and gown.

Nationally, under federal law, a student is supposed to have a transition plan in place during the school year when the student turns 16. In New York State, it's even earlier, the school year when the student turns 15. In Connecticut, conditions for a successful transition start with 14 as the trigger age to commence transition planning in earnest.

There are some states that actually have good transition supports, but the problem is that the supports are not as "well-coordinated," as they are required to be. It does not help the student living in Niagara Falls if the New York state location for a particular type of vocational training or assessment is in Schenectady, more than a four-hour drive away. Most states do not go through the trouble of connecting the transition "dots" so the consumer can make informed choices.

Transition planning while your child is still in the public-school system starts with assessments of your child's strengths and interests. It continues with the development of transition goals and other related supports that reflect an outcome-oriented process facilitating the child's transition from public school to post-secondary life. When students graduate, they should be able to graduate *to* a life that is meaningful and fulfilling.

The most important piece of the transition puzzle is what happens (or does not happen) when the student is still receiving services mandated by the IEP. This is where the foundation for transition is developed and put in place. This section of the IEP is left blank for years and all of a sudden, the time comes when it needs to be filled out.

When we speak of IEP mandates, we're talking about entitlements. So, while the student still has a viable IEP, what are those entitlements? There are quite a few. In New York State, every student with an IEP has the right (but not the obligation) to:

1. Receive transition services in their IEP starting by age 15 or even younger if recommended by the student's IEP team.
2. Receive services through the end of the school year when they turn 21 or until receiving a regular high school diploma.
3. Participate in all IEP meetings (this may not be warranted).
4. Assist in the development of IEP accommodations and modifications.
5. Develop measurable, realistic, and specific post-school outcome goal statements that represent the targets being pursued.

6. Receive transition services and supports to help prepare the student to meet goals for post-secondary education, training, employment, and skills to support independent living.
7. Assist developing goals and objectives to support health care, transportation, self-determination, and social skills.
8. Identify and connect with outside agencies.
9. Be informed by the student's 17th birthday that, subject to a guardianship order from the court, all parental rights will transition to the student by age 18.
10. Assist in planning to address career, academic, and behavioral skills to prepare for post-secondary living.
11. Receive other information regarding IEPs as may be developed by the State Education Department.

If a school district is not honoring the above entitlements, the student has the right to file for mediation or for a due process hearing.

My sense is that, probably due to a lack of adequate training, far too many school districts botch or gloss over the transition process. They pay lip service to transition with generic statements in the IEP such as "when John turns 21, he will pursue employment in accordance with his interests." Or, they might make a statement in the IEP that presumes the child is going on to college and does not need any post-secondary planning.

What if John is not able to be successful at college but has other interests and skill sets that could still make him highly employable and marketable? Did he ever receive meaningful vocational or employment training? All too often the answer is no.

The Empire State Building

You may have heard the story of the poor soul who leaps off the Empire State Building without a parachute. As the man hurtles past the tenth floor, another man sitting at an open window calls out, "Hey man, how's it going?" The jumper smiles, gives the thumbs up sign and cheerily replies "So far, so good!" The joke is on the jumper's misplaced optimism because we know exactly what is going to happen next, and it's not pretty.

The visual of the man hurtling to the sidewalk below is a metaphor for the many thousands of students in public school programs whose parents may be *thinking* "so far so good" but who, in actuality, are facing the imminent loss of valuable entitlements under the federal IDEA statute when they transition to adulthood.

Each year, educational entitlements under the federal IDEA statute will come to a crashing halt at age 21, and sometimes earlier, for many thousands of Americans. This abrupt change in available supports is often referred to as "going off the services cliff." When families reach this precarious juncture, many of them are going over that cliff with limited options and resources that vary widely from state to state.

While there always are plenty of exceptions, when your child goes over the services cliff, you may experience a smoother landing if you are living in states such as New York, Connecticut, Massachusetts, New Jersey, or California. This is not to say that quality adult services are *easy* to secure in the above states, but rather that relative to many other states, these four states may offer more support.

Families who will face the services cliff and its protracted delays when their children exit the public educational system must advocate effectively for educational entitlements, in a timely manner *long before* the cliff appears on the horizon. Parents also need to plan for their child's future by registering with OPWDD and other state agencies.

Transition planning and training should answer some important questions. Where is the student going to live? What are the student's interests? What vocational training would be appropriate? What are the student's prospects for employment or volunteerism? What about participation in social groups? What skills need to be acquired for independent living? It is essential that families and transition professionals get on the same page about what the transition goals are and what progress can be realistically expected.

There is no such thing as the perfect IEP, but it is essential that parents enforce unfulfilled IEP service mandates—even if the services cliff is a long way off. Parents need to ensure that core recommendations made by assessment professionals are implemented meaningfully through the IEP process.

Above all, while your child is still receiving services from the local school district, it is essential that the IEP visibly promote increasing levels of independence and self-sufficiency with goals that are genuinely ambitious, challenging, and take the student's potential into account. Making sure your child gets what he or she is entitled to during the school experience is part of building the transition process—just as pouring a foundation is an important part of building a home. The transition process is one that begins in a bureaucracy of *entitlement* and ends in a bureaucracy of *eligibility*.

If you live in New York State, do not wait until graduation day to register with state agencies such as the OPWDD (Office for People With Developmental Disabilities) or ACCES—VR (Adult Career and Continuing Education Services—Vocational Rehabilitation).[83] Similarly, do not wait until graduation to teach basic daily living skills such as personal hygiene, food preparation, dressing and undressing, having a functional system of communication, and doing the laundry or dishes. Early acquisition of those skills may mean the difference between the student who resides and works as an adult in their community and one who may require a more restrictive and supported setting.

If there is one certainty in the transition process, it is that you will be spending a great deal of time on the phone, initiating or following up with the many functionaries that may or may not be of assistance. Your most valuable investment may just be a $.99 notebook: No matter who you speak with, note the call, the substance of the conversation, the name of the person you spoke with, and any telephone numbers you dialed or were given for future reference. Your trusty notebook will become a resource you will turn to again and again.

If your family lives in New York State, the Office for People With Developmental Disabilities (OPWDD) is the state agency that provides programs and oversees the funding of agencies that provide services to people with developmental disabilities. OPWDD provides a wide variety of support and service options that can be tailored to address an individual's needs. I encourage all New Yorkers to log onto OPWDD's user-friendly website (www.opwdd.ny.gov), which describes "person-centered planning" with supports and services that may include:

✓ Help for living in a home in the local community

✓ Support to live in their family home with supports

---

[83] New York State is finally getting on the transition bandwagon in a real way. For the first time in years, ACCES-VR has established and entered into new contracts with agencies that are able to provide transition services to students.

- ✓ Help for people who want to work in the community and
- ✓ Help for those who need intensive residential and day services

I cannot emphasize enough that families living in New York State should register with OPWDD early on. There are agencies that will provide free evaluations to determine whether a child is eligible for OPWDD's umbrella of supports and services. In Manhattan, these agencies include the Young Adult Institute (YAI) (212-273-6182) and AHRC (212-780-4491). In addition to OPWDD's website, you can also call OPWDD's information hotline (1-866-946-9733).

Assuming that your child meets eligibility requirements and has a qualifying diagnosis that affects independent living, services can include: counseling, respite, recreation, sibling support groups, training, adaptive devices, behavioral services, supported employment opportunities, job coaching, social skills training, equipment, and more.

Most OPWDD services are funded through Medicaid by way of a "Medicaid Waiver." It's considered a waiver system because it does not consider parental income. If your parents happen to be Bill and Melinda Gates, you can still qualify for the waiver if you meet the eligibility criteria.

Before receiving any Medicaid-funded services through OPWDD, an applicant must arrange for a review of records showing evidence of a qualifying disability that arose before age 22; a disability that is serious enough to affect your child's ability to live independently. For eligibility purposes, OPWDD will be looking for a diagnosis of one or more of the following: intellectual disability, autism, epilepsy, cerebral palsy, and certain neurological impairments.

The documents OPWDD will be looking for and reviewing are:

- ✓ OPWDD's eligibility form (available online)
- ✓ A psychological assessment less than three years old that includes adaptive behavior scales and a written summary by the person who did the testing
- ✓ A social or psychosocial history
- ✓ A medical report less than one year old
- ✓ Other documents specifically requested by OPWDD, such as an IEP

The Medicaid Waiver is also sometimes referred to as an HCBS (Home and Community Based Services) Waiver. It is worth repeating that a parent's income is entirely irrelevant to the process: The focus is on the child's income and in many instances, the child doesn't have an income. As an added bonus, if your child is declared to be eligible for the Medicaid waiver, at age 18, the Medicaid waiver magically converts into standard Medicaid for your child without having to go through a separate application process. If, however, you don't have the Medicaid waiver in hand when your child turns 18, you will have to file a separate application.

Why is that? The answer is that once children age out of educational programs, Medicaid benefits are needed for their acceptance into adult programs. The bottom line is that parents have every incentive to explore eligibility under the Medicaid waiver program early on to benefit from services in the near-term, as well as to prepare for the ultimate transition to adulthood.

Currently, Medicaid waiver funding can cover a wide range of services through OPWDD including but not limited to summer and other special needs recreational programs, music and arts programs, parent training and consultation, behavioral services, support groups for parents and siblings, physical therapy, nurses, occupational therapy, medical and dental services, equipment and devices, transportation, respite services, and community programs.

The Medicaid waiver emphasizes person-centered planning—planning in which the child's family members and service providers focus on the child's desires and interests for their future. The waiver also is the mechanism for the child to receive federal and state funds to pay for necessary services that are designed to empower the child so they might live at home, reside in the local community, and have a meaningful and fulfilling life.

Initially, OPWDD must determine whether a person is eligible for its services. This is an administrative determination based on the results of an evaluation and a review of the individual's application and related submissions. OPWDD offers free evaluations through certain agencies. You can submit your application to your local DDRO (Developmental Disability Regional Office) for your borough or during your attendance at one of OPWDD's mandated "front door" information sessions, a helpful and informative presentation that will require about two hours of your time.

Once OPWDD makes an eligibility determination, parents will need to select a Care Coordinator from an approved care coordination agency. There are three care coordination firms that parents can choose from: Advanced Care Alliance, Care Design, and Tri-County Care. The application process can take time—another big reason for parents to apply early.

The application process starts with a telephone call to OPWDD's intake number at (631) 434-6000 and a follow up telephone call from intake personnel to commence the eligibility and enrollment process. One of the important eligibility factors that OPWDD looks at is your child's level of independence. It is important to answer these questions truthfully and be mindful not to inadvertently overstate your child's level of independence. Independence for eligibility purposes means that your child can reliably perform the task at issue on their own without any support or additional prompting from you. If you brag about how independent your child is and they are not genuinely independent, eligibility can be denied on that basis.

There is at least one, and possibly as many as three steps to determine OPWDD eligibility. A face-to-face meeting may be required as part of this process. If, by the third review level, an applicant still has not been declared eligible, the applicant may request a "fair hearing."

Parents who are thinking about registering with OPWDD and learning about its "front door" need to attend one of the OPWDD informational workshops sponsored by your local DDRO (Developmental Disabilities Regional Office). Each borough of New York City has its own DDRO office. In Manhattan, parents can call 646-766-3220 to sign up for an upcoming workshop. The workshop presentation will review the eligibility process and advise families where they can access assistance and the types of services that are available.

Once you receive the letter confirming that your child has met the eligibility requirements, things can really begin to move. You will need to call your local DDRO to ask for a phone interview by an OPWDD Front Door Representative. This phone interview is a very important part of the process and you will be expected to go into detail as to your child's unique needs. Parents who live in Manhattan can call 646-766-3220 to set up this interview.

After eligibility is established, you will need to choose a Care Coordinator who can assist you with the various applications, identify suitable programs, and prepare the service plans that will benefit your child. One of the more important things that the Care Coordinator can do for you is help you apply for the Medicaid Waiver.

Once your child qualifies for the Medicaid Waiver, you may want to consider moving into a program called "self-direction." Some years ago, New York State had 35,000 adults living in group homes. This was one-sixth of the total group home residents in the whole country; New York realized that it was spending 40% more than even California was spending. In addition to what New York was spending on operating and sustaining these group homes, there were some other serious problems, including instances of sexual abuse and other assaults. All of the above precipitated a move by New York to close down and otherwise move away from the group home[84] model in favor of a "self-direction" or consumer-oriented model that would allow a family or agency to construct a customized program and budget around the needs of the individual.

To enroll in OPWDD's self-direction option, you must first work with your Care Coordinator and attend mandatory training sessions. Ultimately, should you choose the self-direction route and qualify for that change, your Care Coordinator will then cease to act in that capacity because you will now be in charge of implementing the budget OPWDD gives you to provide your child's services. Some families prefer having the control that self-direction offers. Other families feel more comfortable continuing with a Care Coordinator. It all depends on what you are up for. Some families have the skill sets for self-direction and some do not.

Self-direction makes you your own UBER driver in charge of managing your adult program and expenditures from an approved budget. As part of this process, it is first necessary to develop and obtain approval for a self-direction budget. It is not unusual for self-direction budgets to be in the six-figure range. The average adult in New York State receives about $90,000 per year for services, with allocations that can range up to $240,000 per year.[85]

Once the self-direction budget is approved, the family can purchase services directly from a provider agency (at the agency's rates) or may choose to hire and train their own staff, at negotiated rates.

Services that are available in the context of self-direction programs include but are not limited to supported employment, respite, and having a live-in caregiver. The budget, subject to limitations, can also cover individual services such as laundry, transportation, camp, health club memberships, parent training, and even massages.

This brings up another serious eligibility issue that parents should carefully watch for at all stages of the process. You don't want to have your child declared ineligible for government funding because he or she has too much money in their own name in a bank or investment house. Make sure to discuss this issue with your counsel, who may advise you to create a "Supplemental Needs Trust" so that this pitfall can be avoided.

There are some private not-for-profits that can supplement the transition support that the public-school system and state agencies are supposed to provide. In New York

---

[84] Group homes are also sometimes referred to as IRAs (individual residential alternatives).
[85] Noah Remnick, "The Coming Care Crisis as Kids With Autism Grow Up," (*The Atlantic*, February 2019).

City, for example, Job Path has been successful for more than 40 years in matching the needs of employers with the skill sets of individuals with autism and other developmental disabilities.

There really is no perfect recipe to make the transition soufflé. Every individual will present with unique needs and the resources available in adulthood will vary tremendously from state to state. Whatever you do, earlier is better. At the end of the day, it is incumbent upon all concerned to work collaboratively toward a good outcome.

Chapter 14
Confronting Bullying and Discrimination in the Workplace

Until the COVID-19 pandemic arrived, the employment landscape had been improving somewhat for individuals with disabilities. Yet, in any economy, it is incredibly challenging for a person on the autism spectrum to find gainful employment. The latest statistics indicate that the unemployment rate for the autism population hovers around 85%. When a pandemic is not causing a 20% unemployment rate for the neurotypical population,[86] normally that 85% compares to about a 4% or 5% unemployment rate for the general population.

As difficult as it may be for a person on the spectrum to *find* a decent job, it is a cinch to *lose* a position of employment due to social or political factors having little, if anything, to do with the employee's competence or job performance. Unfortunately, the bullying and negative attitudes that surface in school settings can also arise in the workplace.

The court's decision in one of our most memorable cases, *New York City Housing Authority v. Peter Hightower*, illustrates this important lesson. Our client, Peter Hightower, had been employed for many years by the New York City Housing Authority as a custodian. Mr. Hightower's job was based on the grounds of a public housing project and his primary duties involved mopping out the elevators and waste management. Mr. Hightower was proud to be employed. His mother was even prouder.

---

[86] During the Great Depression, the unemployment rate was approximately 24%.

With Peter Hightower and his mother

The case involved charges of serious misconduct filed by Mr. Hightower's new supervisor, Ms. D. If the charges were proven, Mr. Hightower would likely be fired, so a lot was at stake. We offered to take the case pro bono after meeting Mr. Hightower and his mother.

We learned that Mr. Hightower had a spotless employment record as a Housing Authority custodian for more than eight years. He had developed an excellent working relationship with his prior supervisor and also decent relationships with many, but apparently not all, of his fellow custodians. Mr. Hightower disclosed the fact that he had been diagnosed on the autism spectrum.

A few of Mr. Hightower's coworkers resented the fact that they were assigned to work with someone like him (i.e. someone with a developmental disability) being paid at the same rate. These coworkers apparently were looking for an opportunity—any opportunity—to get rid of Mr. Hightower. That opportunity arrived soon after Ms. D became Mr. Hightower's new supervisor.

One afternoon, two of Mr. Hightower's coworkers told Ms. D that she needed to be "careful" because they allegedly heard Mr. Hightower threatening to hurt her when she clocked out at the end of the workday. The same coworkers then threw gasoline on this already explosive situation. They told Ms. D that they heard Mr. Hightower making derogatory comments about the shape and size of her breasts.

That was all Ms. D had to hear. She filed formal charges against Mr. Hightower, alleging that he had threatened to harm her. Mr. Hightower flatly denied the charges and entered a plea of not guilty. This forced the Housing Authority's counsel to call some of Mr.

Hightower's coworkers as witnesses. Mr. Hightower's heart sank when we showed him the Housing Authority's witness list. It was difficult for him to understand or believe that any of his coworkers would want to testify against him.

The judge granted our motion to sequester all witnesses to prevent any witness from hearing any other witness's testimony. This turned out to be a critical event because the coworkers who signed up to testify against Mr. Hightower could not keep their stories straight. These coworkers wanted to get rid of Mr. Hightower so badly, they outdid each other giving completely *different* accounts of the threats allegedly made by Mr. Hightower.

One of the Housing Authority's witnesses testified that Mr. Hightower had threatened to slap Ms. D "in her face." The next witness called by the Housing Authority, however, claimed that Mr. Hightower threatened to "stab and kill" Ms. D. The story further deteriorated when the Housing Authority's third witness took the witness stand, claiming that Mr. Hightower had threatened to "smack the shit out of" Ms. D.

When Mr. Hightower's mother Phyllis took the witness stand, she spoke of her own run-in with Ms. D. Apparently, Ms. D had suggested that people with disabilities should work "elsewhere." There was evidence that Ms. D was especially difficult and demanding and that she deliberately confused Mr. Hightower by asking him to perform several tasks at the same time. Mr. Hightower's mother also spoke of teasing and bullying by some coworkers. Ms. D's dismissive response was that Mr. Hightower "was a man who could stand up for himself." In other words, Ms. D had little interest in becoming involved.

One of the Housing Authority's assistant supervisors had the courage and integrity to confirm the extent of the teasing and bullying—and that Ms. D and a number of Mr. Hightower's coworkers wanted him to be transferred to another custodial unit.

Because of what the trial judge referred to as the "many differing versions" offered by the Housing Authority's witnesses and the evidence of animosity toward Mr. Hightower, the trial judge ruled that the Housing Authority's key witnesses were lacking in credibility and therefore the Housing Authority failed to prove its case. Accordingly, the trial judge ruled that Mr. Hightower was not guilty of any conduct warranting the termination of his employment. Today, years later, Mr. Hightower still has his job.[87]

The takeaway from the *Hightower* case is that the bullying and related abuse that can occur in school settings can also occur in the workplace as a form of discrimination. In an abundance of caution, the prudent employee will promptly bring such conduct to the

---

[87] Mr. Hightower became a union representative and continues to work for the New York City Housing Authority.

attention of HR and/or to other supervisory personnel, preferably in writing. If the acts complained of continue, it would be advisable to consult with counsel, bearing in mind that it often is easier to *prevent* the termination of employment than it is to restore it.

Employment conflicts can sometimes be averted or neutralized by creative planning at or before the time of hire. Fredda Rosen, the Executive Director of Job Path,[88] a not-for-profit with more than 40 years of experience helping individuals with developmental disabilities join the workforce, says:

"The better the match is at the outset between the employer's needs and the employees' interests and skill sets, the better the chances that the position of employment will be sustainable. An employment opportunity can and should be customized and engineered from a 'strengths' perspective to focus on what the employee is *able* to do versus what tasks may be unduly challenging.

Job Path's philosophy is that there is a job for everyone. Ultimately, however, hiring an individual must make good business sense from the perspective of the employer. No employer, for example, should ever be asked to pay for 'make work' that the employer does not need to be performed. Nor should an employer be expected to continue the employment of an individual whose work does not add value to the employer's operations.

Under our Job Path model, a great deal of training time is invested in the beginning of the employment relationship at no cost to the employer. This approach is designed to ensure a good fit. That fit, coupled with our ongoing job coaching support, pays off in the long run for all concerned."

In the decades to come, more and more individuals with autism will have the opportunity to be gainfully employed as they transition to adulthood. As explained in Chapter 13 (page 135), these opportunities will bear a direct relationship to the extent that students are able to timely access the various "transition" entitlements mandated in the applicable statutes.

After employment commences, it is essential to remain vigilant for any "red flags" that might signal the need for appropriate intervention or redirection. Many of these red flags are similar to the warning signs that parents need to be alert to when bullying is going on at school:

---

[88] In the interests of full disclosure, I serve as Job Path's Board Chair.

- ✓ When you ask your son or daughter about what's going on at work, they "don't want to talk about it"
- ✓ Excessive absences and lateness
- ✓ Mood changes
- ✓ Weight swings
- ✓ Your son or daughter wants to "change jobs" but gives no reason
- ✓ Supervisor turnover
- ✓ Your child is repeatedly being "written up" for alleged infractions
- ✓ Instances of property loss or destruction
- ✓ Moved to undesirable shifts
- ✓ Change to unpleasant assignments and tasks
- ✓ Exclusion from office activities that others participate in
- ✓ Other evidence of a "hostile environment"

Chapter 15
Guardianship, Special Needs Trusts, and Powers of Attorney

If your child is eight years old and breaks an arm running around the local playground, the hospital's doctors will turn to you as the parent to make medical decisions and give or withhold consent. If, on the other hand, your child is 18, you will lose that decision-making authority unless a court has appointed you as legal guardian, you have a power of attorney (or health proxy) duly executed by your child, or your child has consented to the guardianship application.

Many parents who have children diagnosed with ASD will easily meet the test for a general guardianship, or at least for a limited guardianship that gives the parent decision-making power over particular activities. Other parents, however, will not be able to meet the test to be appointed as their child's guardian to any extent. The core issue is whether or not the court concludes that your child is "incapacitated" or "impaired" in the sense that they are not able to manage their own affairs or understand the nature and consequences of their decisions. Ironically, the fact that some parents will not be able to meet that test is a *positive* reflection of their child's level of independence.

The test is not simply that your ASD child would likely make bad decisions. There are plenty of neurotypical individuals who make poor, if not disastrous, life choices. (Think of the person who drains out the cash equity in their home with a second mortgage and then blows that cash gambling in Las Vegas.) Ordinarily, the courts will allow neurotypical people to literally ruin their lives without appointing a guardian or conservator.

Sometimes, the incapacity/impairment issue is clear. If, however, you are the parent of a verbal, higher-functioning child on the autism spectrum, you might not qualify for guardianship unless your child consents to that status. Even without a guardianship order, a detailed, comprehensive power of attorney can provide you with the same level of protection and peace of mind. A health proxy signed by your child can also be helpful, at least for medical treatment issues.

When your child transitions to adulthood, the ability to receive services and other governmental benefits may be adversely impacted if your child has too much money in his or her name, in a bank or brokerage account. Many parents avoid this kind of pitfall by working with their attorneys to create a Special Needs Trust, provided that such a trust complies with the necessary requirements. Establishing a Special Needs Trust is something that parents will likely want to do earlier than later; consult with your attorney.

The caveat is that if you are the parent who may need to draw upon and receive federal and state benefits after your child transitions to adulthood, you need to make sure that well-meaning grandparents and other relatives do not make bequests in their wills that would go directly to your child. Thank them for thinking of you and your family but advise them to make the bequest expressly payable to your child's Special Needs Trust. That can eliminate serious problems down the line.

Chapter 16
The Advent of Telehealth Instruction During The COVID-19 Pandemic[89]

The onset of the COVID-19 pandemic compelled a seismic and almost immediate shift in the US education system as the nation's schools were shuttered and millions of students were sent home indefinitely, with no reliable return date in sight. Putting aside for the moment the grim economic, social and employment consequences, school districts and private schools throughout the nation scrambled in an effort to make the best of what was left of the 2019-2020 school year.

Guidance from the Centers for Disease Control and Prevention (CDC) and World Health Organization (WHO) to slow the spread of COVID-19, coupled with strategies for social distancing and government orders to stay at home, meant that few options remained for providing instruction. For typically developing learners, this largely translated to distance learning incorporating synchronous, or live teaching sessions via remote video or asynchronous learning (recorded video/no real-time interaction) with written assignments that would heavily incorporate the use of relatively inexpensive and widely accessible technology.[90]

For students with disabilities, however, the process of transferring a student's Individualized Education Plan (IEP) to a similar model proved to be more problematic. At its core, this transfer necessarily entails a concept that is central to the most important

---

[89] I acknowledge, with thanks, the many significant contributions of Dr. Amy Davies-Lackey, Ph.D, BCBA-D, LBA-NY in the development of this chapter and the "generalization" section of the Appendix. At the time this book is going to press, the nation's schools are still closed and, in the main, are not expected to reopen before the start of the 2020-2021 school year.

[90] The adaptation to "telehealth" technology quickly spilled over into my law practice, as perhaps the perfect response and antidote to social distancing, office closures and the fact that most client families, overnight, were sheltering at and working from home.

mandates of the IDEA statute- equitable access to instruction, and the appropriateness of that instruction. As noted earlier, remote teaching is not so much about attendance as it is about attending.

There is a growing literature base for determining the appropriateness of the telehealth model (Rodriguez, in press) when it comes to insurance-based practice. However, the models for such programs within the school setting are limited. What happens during a pandemic where synchronous video conferencing direct instruction is the *only* option due to social distancing requirements? What are the ethical and educational ramifications of disruptions to critical educational and therapeutic services?

Synchronous Video Instruction

While shifting from in-person/class delivery of instruction to synchronous video instruction is less than ideal, it is feasible when *individually* tailored to the needs of the learner and the learner's family. Even a pandemic does not excuse inappropriate, "one size fits all" programming. Behavior analysts and educators have a responsibility to ensure that the programs they develop are reasonably calculated to generate a significant and meaningful educational benefit for the student. To achieve this for learners with intensive needs, it is necessary to reexamine the delivery vehicle frequently to make sure that it is achieving its objective. Educating students with intensive learning and behavioral needs, however, goes beyond a shift to remote instruction.

As one might expect, the students presenting with the greatest challenges in delivering synchronous video instruction also are the ones most in need of the services- students who present with challenges in attending, joint attention skills, communication skills and often intensive behavior needs. In shifting from a direct instruction model to a remote instruction platform, a critical factor is the ability and capacity of the client to attend to and respond to skill acquisition programs. For some students, this extends to building foundational skills for remote instruction.

Synchronous video instruction allows teachers to deliver one-to-one or small group instruction through a live video feed. Students with intensive instructional needs require a parent to act as a proxy for the teacher. In essence, the parent functions as the "hands" of the teacher, providing prompting and reinforcement opportunities as needed. This approach requires teachers to exercise flexibility, consistency and thoughtfulness in their instructional delivery, coaching of parents, and data collection.

A Durability Test For Generalization

Remote instruction simultaneously presents opportunities and challenges for students with autism. This format of instruction represents the ultimate test of functionality and the generalization of skills. Can the student demonstrate the skills that are being taught in the natural environment, and even under situations of stress?

With remote instruction, parents are prematurely thrown into the deep end of the pool and directed to swim. It is, however, a critical teaching opportunity to take advantage of. It also is a chance to observe, educate and provide feedback to parents in real-time.

So many students fall off of the proverbial "services cliff" when they transition to adulthood and their IDEA-based programs come to a screeching halt. Being thrust into remote instruction presents an opportunity to acquire at least some of the transition skills they will need later on.

Measuring the Effectiveness of Programming

It is not enough to simply provide the services. Special care must be given to properly measure the *effectiveness* of teaching. For individualized and group teaching sessions, data can be collected contemporaneously through captured discrete trial, permanent products, fluency measures and other dimensions of measurement. Parent education entails a more complex, but equally valuable form of measurement. This can include discrete measurement such as the number of prompts provided to the parent during synchronous teaching sessions where the parent is a "proxy" or permanent products produced by the parent (such as the programming of an assistive technology device) that relate to progress made with the student.

Flexibility in Providing Intensive and Multifaceted Family Supports

Quarantine orders that issued during the COVID-19 outbreak helped to create a "perfect storm" for families who may need access to crisis services or additional supports in caring for their child. Parents manage multiple contingencies – stressful jobs, instability in their employment and income, multiple children with instructional needs, limited technology access, and, of course, having and educating a child with a disability. Achieving the right balance of services and supports is key in maintaining safety.

Considerations must also be made during quarantine for how to effectively support the inevitable crises that may arise. In a time where community supports are not readily available and a 911 visit to the hospital may have grave consequences, professionals must ready families with a support network and the skills to execute said assistance when needed. What is the plan when the parent or other caregiver becomes ill and has to be rushed to the hospital? What is the plan if the parent supporting the student's remote learning program is supposed to be working all day from home? Can the caregiver execute a behavior plan without supports when a crisis occurs outside of normal "working" hours? Can they manage a situation where the 911 response is delayed due to being overwhelmed by emergency calls? Can they mitigate problem behavior when the risks associated with a hospital visit are too high?

Documenting Attendance And Progress For Reimbursement Purposes

Aside from the clinical considerations, how should a parent being asked to serve as the teacher's surrogate in a remote "tele" teaching program document the student's attendance, participation and progress? This question is particularly relevant for parents who have filed or are thinking of filing for an impartial hearing. In most cases, parents filed for their hearing long before COVID-19 arrived and long before the school system closed and remote teaching, by default, became the order of the day.

Parents should maintain a written chronology and schedule of all teaching sessions, including the provision of any related services. The parent and the student's school should agree on a format for collecting data on the student's participation and progress. To the extent feasible, schools should develop a "remote learning plan" that conforms to the reasonable expectations of the school system. In this connection, parents who are supporting remote teaching should consider taking and preserving short video segments showing their child's participation and involvement in instructional opportunities. This can be accomplished via any smartphone. If needed, educational consultants can also be engaged to review the appropriateness of the student's remote program.

Ultimately, our nation's students will return to school in the classic sense and anxious parents, teachers and administrators will breathe at least a half sigh of relief. When they do, particularly for parent training, social skills training, group instruction, probing for generalization and the like, we can expect a significant level of remote "tele" learning to remain embedded in the nation's educational repertoire.

References

Rodriguez, K. (2020, March 30). Maintaining Treatment Integrity in the Face of Crisis: A Treatment Selection Model for Transitioning Direct ABA Services to Telehealth. https://doi.org/10.31234/osf.io/phtgv

Chapter 17
The Road Ahead—Institutionalizing High Expectations and Discontent

When parents first receive their child's autism diagnosis, they often pray for relatively small miracles. "If only Elizabeth could speak and call me mama." "If only Michael could learn in a regular classroom like everyone else." "If only Jared could make a friend." "If only Emily could toilet independently."

But when parents and professionals see the very progress they've been hoping for, it is only human nature to ratchet up the previous expectations. If Isabelle can learn five words, then why not 50? When she has the 50 words under her belt, why not 500? Why not 5,000? Discontent and dissatisfaction, coupled with having high-but-realistic expectations, can be a powerful, positive force for learning—and ultimately for achieving greater levels of independence and self-sufficiency.

It may be counterintuitive, but in this context, expressing discontent and dissatisfaction is not "being negative." Put that thought out of your head. Rather, it is intended as hopeful and loving inspiration, much as a professional basketball coach might "give it" to his team trailing by 20 points at halftime, hoping that doing so might wake them up and turn the game around (i.e. turn a negative into a positive).

Charlie Rose once asked Shimon Peres, the former Prime Minister of Israel, why the Jewish people have managed to achieve so much despite their relatively small numbers. Peres credited these achievements to maintaining a state of perpetual discontent and dissatisfaction, saying "The Jews' greatest contribution to history is dissatisfaction. We're a nation born to be discontent. Whatever exists we believe can be changed for the better."[91] Leave it to Israel, then, to have created Unit 900, a special intelligence unit

---
91 This principle is brought to life in a time-worn Miami Beach parable. A grandmother takes her toddler

that actively recruits individuals with autism who have exceptional visual discrimination skills—valuable skills in, for example, comparing before-and-after aerial and satellite photos.

In its most recent reauthorization of the IDEA statute, Congress recognized that having high expectations is a necessary foundation for achieving better outcomes. Indeed, Congress blamed "low expectations" for the IDEA statute not achieving more. It seems that when you shoot for the moon, you actually improve your chances of getting there. On the other hand, having low expectations comes with its own, all-too-predictable outcome: When you aim low, you simply cannot expect to do any better.

Now, of course, we have the benefit of the Supreme Court's unanimous 2017 decision in the *Endrew F.* case. School systems across the nation are required to offer programs that are "ambitious" and "challenging," consistent with the student's unique needs and potential. The Supreme Court's ruling in *Endrew F.*, at least on paper, compels the nation's school districts to systemically implement higher expectations.

Until relatively recently, best-practice teaching approaches such as Applied Behavior Analysis were generally reserved for private schools. While there's still a long way to go, we are seeing many public-school systems across the country adopting, implementing, and "owning" these approaches. Finally, we are beginning to meaningfully *institutionalize* high expectations.

School systems are finally improving transition planning and supports so that when students graduate from the public school system, they can graduate "to" something that is meaningful and fulfilling. In the next decade, as more employers recognize that hiring individuals with autism adds value to the bottom line, the staggering 85% unemployment rate should decline significantly. Yet, even if there is a 50% reduction in the unemployment rate, we can do even better. That is the nature of progress—not allowing ourselves to become content or complacent as long as there is something else that can be done to make things better.

While social-skills training has long been available for individuals with autism who need to develop better communication and socialization skills, there are now autism

---

grandson to the beach. As the grandson is sitting at the water's edge, shoveling sand into a plastic pail, a rogue wave appears out of nowhere, swallowing the toddler and taking him out to sea. The distraught grandmother beseeches God. "Oh God, you must help me. If you will only return my grandson safe and sound, I'll never, ever ask you for anything again. My daughter is going to kill me. Please—I beg of you." At that moment, another rogue wave appears, this time returning the grandson without so much as a scratch. Even his plastic pail and shovel have been returned. The toddler resumes shoveling sand into his pail. The grandmother looks up at the sky with a sour facial expression and says, "He had a hat."

dating sites and "meetups." Not too long ago, the prospect of developing and sustaining a relationship was quite remote. Today, individuals with autism are just as likely as their parents to be reading informative and helpful "how to" books such as *Decoding Dating*, by John Miller.

Within the next decade, I believe there will be school systems restructuring their teaching programs to give far greater priority to social skills and the need for ASD students to generalize the many skills they ostensibly are learning. I think we are also going to see school systems finally address transition supports and vocational training as Congress intended. To be sure, inasmuch as there is nothing more important than saving lives and preserving the public health, the COVID-19 pandemic will inspire or compel numerous profound changes in our school and classroom environments, as well as available teaching approaches.

Finally, if recent history is any guide, many more colleges, universities, and employers will develop and implement the accommodations and programs needed to support students with ASD. The road ahead to greater levels of independence will likely be a lot smoother for the generations to come.

It is incredibly gratifying to see what some of our early "preschooler" clients have managed to achieve. One, "B," is graduating this year from MIT (virtually because of the pandemic) and has been accepted to graduate school for physics at Carnegie Mellon. Another, "J," recently graduated from the University of Michigan. I think of how incredibly far those students have come. And yet, because autism is a spectrum disorder, we must bear in mind that progress is always relative. It is far less about what a student achieves and much more about what a student is able to overcome. Accordingly, let me be the first to say that the achievements and progress of those who do *not* go on to a college or grad school experience are just as important and praiseworthy as the achievements of those who are able to distinguish themselves academically.

Even with excellent potential, perhaps the most important predictor of a good outcome is how the time leading up to the student's transition to adulthood has been spent and invested. Autism is an enigmatic disorder operating in an equally enigmatic and uncertain world. Accordingly, whatever an individual's ultimate potential might be, and whatever may be the state of the world at any given moment, if we have diligently harnessed our expectations and discontent in a concerted effort to attain greater levels of independence and self-sufficiency, we will have done our job.

PART II

Advice From the Experts

Appendix A

Teaching Generalization For a More Independent and Enriched Life
By Dr. Amy Davies-Lackey, BCBA, LBA

As parents and educators, we guide students to apply the skills we teach as a means to an end: leading an independent and fulfilling life. The many hours (and dollars) spent teaching strategies and skills are done with the intention of helping students become employed, live as independently as possible, and become effective communicators—no matter where their paths take them. Achieving this goal requires targeted programming for generalization.

Over the past 10–20 years, service delivery for individuals with autism spectrum disorders has shifted to reflect the growing literature on the concept of generalization within the applied behavior analysis (ABA) field. Early applications of ABA often included discrete trial instruction. This type of instruction is characterized by highly structured teaching sessions providing ample opportunities to practice skills; measurable, observable, and definable teaching objectives; clear and concise data collection and analysis; and teaching practices steeped in reinforcement opportunities (Sundberg & Partington, 1998). However, the highly structured nature of discrete trial instruction, left in untrained hands, can result in teaching that does not program for generalization but instead results in overly specific stimulus control or prompt dependence.

While the days of discrete trial instruction are not gone, there has been a marked shift in the application of the science to reflect instruction provided within the natural environment. The assumption that students will automatically apply the skills we teach is an antiquated view which has been demystified over decades of research (Marini & Genereux, 1995). Examples of naturalistic applications of ABA principles include Early Start Denver Model (Schriebman et al, 2015), Natural Language Paradigm (Koegel, O'Dell, & Koegel, 1987), and Pivotal Response Training (Koegel, Koegel, & Brookman, 2003). Each of these models integrate methods for increasing motivation and generalization through incorporating the child's interests into teaching sessions not limited to discrete trial instruction in treatment.

Generality of behavior change is one of the seven defining characteristics of ABA (Baer, Wolf, & Risley, 1968). Within this broad topic, Stokes & Baer (1977) identified key considerations in programming for generalization across time, settings, persons, and behaviors: introducing natural maintaining contingencies, training sufficient exemplars, training loosely, using indiscriminable contingencies, programming common stimuli, mediating generalization, and training "to generalize" (Stokes & Baer, 1977, 46-47).

Each of these well-researched strategies fall within two primary domains: stimulus generalization and response generalization.

For stimulus generalization, behaviors of interest include responses to stimuli or materials not used in direct instruction. Stimulus generalization occurs when stimuli sharing similar physical properties with the controlling antecedent stimulus evoke a response (Cooper et. al, 2007). As an example, it is common for young learners who are taught to identify "mom"—but will also call a teacher or a female neighbor "mom." Programming that addresses the critical features and further discriminations can promote a different degree of stimulus control.

By contrast, response generalization involves topographically dissimilar but functionally equivalent behaviors in response to stimuli. Meaning, the behavior looks different, but the outcome is the same. Given how rapidly technology is evolving, it is essential that individuals learn target behaviors for new stimuli. Take for instance, a bathroom sink: to properly turn on the water to wash your hands, some faucets require the handles turned, some need to be pushed, and others are turned on by a sensor you wave your hand in front of. The response results in functionally similar outcomes, but the behavior looks different, depending on the technology.

Students with autism spectrum disorders may acquire a multitude of skills in the classroom, but if they are unable to generalize these skills to real life, we have failed them as educators. To be effective, behavior change must be sustainable across persons, time, and settings—and across a number of related behaviors. How do we address these deficits? The key lies within well-established, linear programming that incorporates generalization from the onset.

Generalization Map with the End Result in Mind

Since generalization is a critical feature of independence, programming for generalized behavior change is an essential treatment component. Establishing a "roadmap" for each program can be useful to ensure functionality for the student and program for generalized outcomes. When conceptualizing the structure of programming (taking into consideration the techniques outlined by Stokes & Baer), it's essential to start with an outline of how and when the skill will be used in the future. What is the end goal? Will it functionally produce reinforcement for the individual?

Beginning with the end goal and working backward to establish short-term objectives allows for sequential modification and programming. As these goals are scripted out, fading reinforcement schedules and fluent performance of the skill should be considered. Failure to properly strengthen the performance of a response under natural contingencies of reinforcement virtually guarantees that the skill will be unlikely to persist over time with little to no practice.

Special emphasis on "variety" is essential to effectively combining generalized effects across time, settings, and behaviors. Providing variety within programming should include varying the teaching materials, training settings, the people present when performing the skill, and even being able to discriminate when *not* to perform the skill.

Persistence in performance is often the key to job success. Can the individual keep working without a job coach or supervisor present? Will they keep working when reinforcement has been faded to scheduled breaks or a biweekly paycheck? Can they work among the distractions of a busy office? Can they discriminate when *not* to engage in specific behaviors? Essential considerations in programming include how the skill needs to be performed, when it should be performed, with whom it should be performed, and what that behavior or skill will look like in the context of the community or workplace.

Transdisciplinary Collaboration (Therapists and Parents)

Assuming the role of the "superman" teacher or therapist is a dangerous undertaking that often fails to result in robust outcomes for students. Regular transdisciplinary collaboration provides multidimensional professional expertise on programming for generalization. This transdisciplinary team must include several key stakeholders: teachers, therapists, and (very critical players) the parents.

With roughly 50,000 students with autism transitioning into adulthood every year, it is critical that parents and caregivers are involved in the teaching process. As students age into adulthood, we must provide the tools to promote generalization years before students leave the proverbial "schoolhouse doors." Empowering parents and caregivers to teach, maintain, and promote generalization is a cornerstone of successful transition into adulthood. In school, we will never be able to teach all the skills our students will need in adulthood; parents and caregivers need to know how to carry on that legacy in the next chapter of their child's life.

Structured, frequent team meetings are a pivotal starting point in transdisciplinary thinking. Meetings should include goals that transcend teaching and therapy environments—for example, a vocational goal of washing dishes might include input from the behavior analyst on how to task-analyze the skill and adjust or fade the reinforcement schedule. Suggestions from the speech and language pathologist could incorporate communication with the "boss" or job coach using augmentative and alternative communication. Finally, recommendations from the occupational therapist might focus on increasing fluency in the motor movements required for dishwashing, decreasing the risk of repetitive movement injuries or sensory consequences that may inhibit success.

Collaborative programming allows ample opportunities for the student to respond and practice across providers with multiple exemplars; cross domain boundaries that address the student's core deficits; and incorporate multiple perspectives to examine how the student may need to perform the skill in the future.

Student Performance is the "Report Card" for Your Teaching

Inherent in the title "teacher" is the assumption that you have helped someone acquire knowledge. Ensuring that teaching results in lasting benefits is perhaps the most distinguishing feature of this role. The reach of a student's responsiveness to intervention extends far beyond the data collection and analysis of ABA. The key operation across methodologies is how you can assess the outcomes of teaching. A student's failure to perform a skill across persons, settings, and time reflects a shortcoming in *teaching* procedures—not a reflection on the student.

If student success hinges on the acquisition and sustainable generalization of the skills we have taught them, it is incumbent upon teachers to ensure that our instructional approaches, materials, and planning promote generalization. Achieving this goal means we can help ensure that students have the knowledge and application of skills that will serve them in becoming integrated, contributing, and more independent members of their communities.

References

Baer, D. M., Wolf, M. M., & Risley, T. R. (1968). Some current dimensions of applied behavior analysis. *Journal of Applied Behavior Analysis*, 1, 91-97.

Cooper J.O, Heron T.E, & Heward W.L. *Applied Behavior Analysis* (2nd ed.). Upper Saddle River, NJ: Pearson; 2007.

Koegel, R. L., Koegel, L. K., & McNerney, E. K. (2001). Pivotal areas in intervention for autism. *Journal of Clinical Child Psychology*, 30, 19-32.

Koegel, R. L., O'Dell, M. C., & Koegel, L. K. (1987). A natural language teaching paradigm for nonverbal autistic children. *Journal of Autism and Developmental Disabilities*, 17, 187- 200.

Marini, A. & Genereux, R. (1995). The Challenge of Teaching for Transfer. From A. McKeough, J.L. Lupart, A. Marini (Eds.) *Teaching for Transfer: Fostering Generalization in Learning* (pp.1-20). Mahwah, N.J.: Lawrence Erlbaum Associates.

Schreibman, L., Dawson, G., Stahmer, A. C., Landa, R., Rogers, S. J., McGee, G. G., Kasari, C., Ingersoll, B., Kaiser, A.P., Bruinsma, Y., McNerney, E., Wetherby, A. & Halladay, A. (2015). Naturalistic Developmental Behavioral Interventions: Empirically Validated Treatments for Autism Spectrum Disorder. *Journal of Autism and Developmental Disorders*, 45(8), 2411–2428.

Stokes, T. F., & Baer, D. M. (1977). An Implicit Technology of Generalization. *Journal of Applied Behavior Analysis*, 10, 349-367.

Appendix B

Observing and Assessing Mainstream, Inclusion, and Special Education Classrooms—What I Look For
By David Salsberg, Psy.D.

As pediatric neuropsychologists, our arsenal of recommendations needs to embrace the core of any child's developmental growth outside of the family; namely school. We are charged to be as familiar as possible with the wide range of placements, programs, schools, and interventions that can be made available for the children we see. Besides having this knowledge and being able to keep up to date on those resources, it also is our responsibility to understand the applicable rights and laws. It also helps to be familiar with knowledgeable attorneys and others who can help secure these services when they are needed. Not having this breadth of knowledge would drastically diminish the usefulness of our assessments, recommendations, and advocacy.

Conducting an evaluation but then making generic recommendations such as "contact your local district to initiate an IEP meeting" would be like going for a checkup and your doctor saying "it looks like you have an infection and you need some medicine, but go to your pharmacy and ask what they think and how to get it." Families depend on us to make targeted recommendations to address their child's unique needs. A core part of our job, therefore, involves visiting and assessing schools so we can competently make those recommendations.

This section is focused on the range of school placements and programs that may be explored for children on the autism spectrum: a range that comes with its own "spectrum." Rather than examining the structural factors of a school (such as the range of licensing and accreditation), this will focus on clinical impressions. Since there is such a wide disparity of what we see throughout the country, as well as internationally, the emphasis is on what we look for and the pros and cons of different options in relation to a student's needs.

As has been addressed throughout this book, it cannot be stated strongly enough that the autism spectrum is quite broad and those who carry that diagnosis are a genuinely diverse group. Each child will have unique needs and presentations; nothing discussed should be considered applicable to every child. Even programs that are demonstrably appropriate for a child at one point may not be at another stage of their development. Accordingly, every program should be actively monitored and reassessed.

An important lesson I've learned over the years is that even the best programs may not always be able to address every area of parents' concerns, hopes, and priorities. This is a crucial part of my discussions with parents when brainstorming about programs and placements. When assessing a child or a school program recommendation, of course the parents' goals are an important and informative consideration. However, as clinicians, we need to remain objective and may not always agree with everything a parent may wish for.

If there is a poor fit between a school's resources and a child's needs, it is our duty to say so. We are not hired guns; rather, it is our charge to independently, objectively inform parents of our impressions and be open to collaborating to make recommendations and decisions. This issue often comes up when parents tell me that they want their child to be mainstreamed. That goal is often achievable, but some children may benefit from (or require) interventions in a more structured and supportive setting. If this is my conclusion based on the child's needs and the available programs, I will do all I can to help a parent see the possibilities and work toward a decision they are comfortable with. Similarly, if a parent believes their child should be in a more restrictive setting than I do, I will work hard with them to explore and understand the less restrictive options. Above all, I am guided by what is best for the child, after considering all the relevant factors.

With all school options for a child with special needs, the continuum of placements range from least to most restrictive. The primary focus needs to be on how to most appropriately address the child's needs across educational, social, and emotional domains. The crucial first step is a thorough evaluation that assesses the totality of the child's needs. These evaluations should take a holistic approach, looking at the child's strengths and deficits to fully understand what programs would be appropriate.

It is often necessary to see a child a number of times and in a variety of contexts. In addition to formal or informal testing and parent interviews, we will often observe a child in their school, at home or with specific providers, obtain videos, or whatever it takes to get a full sense of the child. Armed with all of this information, the next step is making placement decisions across the continuum from general education to highly restrictive self-contained classes and schools. In some cases, recommendations might be even more restrictive, such as 1:1 or home programs, hospital-based programs, or residential programs.

Again, there is no "one-size fits all" model. And while we all want (and are mandated with) finding the "least restrictive environment" (LRE), even that demands that it be the least restrictive environment that is *appropriate* for the child's specific needs. The goal of this section is to discuss what we look for in the various types of programs.

Looking at General Education and Inclusion Settings

A critical factor in assessing any program is a look from the top-down. Do the professionals making decisions and delivering services appear committed to understanding the nuances of the child, as opposed to acting as though the child *is* the diagnosis or a set of scores? What should be standard practice (and makes the most sense at IEP meetings) is that the team has thoroughly reviewed and assessed the needs of the child and also has direct knowledge and investment in carrying out the services they recommend. IEP teams from different schools or those that simply hand off their program recommendation to a different body for a placement assignment are sometimes less comprehensive in their utility of recommendations.

When we see children with complex needs who may test well or have some academic and social strengths, there is more of a push for general education placement with informal or 504 supports, or an IEP with related services. When this is viable, there are a number of things we look for in public or private schools. An important starting point (one that we have little control over) is the size of the class and student-to-teacher ratio. What are the presenting challenges of the child in terms of attention, sensory needs, and self-regulation—and how will these needs interact in the classroom, which can range in size? If starting with a larger or less restrictive setting, it is important to discuss with the team what level of monitoring or needs assessments are done (and how quickly) so as not to wait to intervene if things get more overwhelming.

In general education or mainstream settings with related services, we look at how these services are delivered and coordinated, for flexibility in push-in or pull-out services, and for openness to considering individual or group services based on the child's specific needs (opposed to staffing and what is most common). If there are pull-out services, how are they coordinated in a thoughtful way so as not to further isolate a child or have them fall behind in another area. It is important to get a sense of how the staff collaborates with each other; how often do they have team meetings or at least communicate regularly to assure consistency of needs and goals?

We also look to see, and encourage, how open staff are to collaborating with outside therapists, professionals, and parents, as appropriate. If the child needs behaviorally driven interventions, who is delivering them and what is their level of experience and/or supervision? The experience and training of the educators and therapists are critical and, again, need to match the child's specific needs. A reading teacher may be appropriate, but if the child needs a highly skilled OG teacher, we need to secure that. The same goes for the range of specific needs, from a child who needs a PROMPT certified SLP to a child who needs a BCBA-level behaviorist or teacher. If a school is committed to truly, appropriately addressing the child's needs, these services should be available, and if not, are they open to securing these services as needed?

This is especially critical when there are more specialized services needed such as assistive technology (AT), augmentative and alternative communication (AAC) and devices, and vision or hearing services. When these services are delivered, appropriate levels of training and intensity of interventions should also be delivered and carried over in the home as part of the educational plan.

In general education school environments, sometimes the school's belief is that their sole focus should be on academics. While academics are important, a major need with children on the Autism spectrum is social and emotional functioning. This has to be incorporated into any educational plan for a child with these needs. In evaluating programs, we look to see who delivers these services and in what contexts. Care and service delivery must be considered throughout the day.

It is often non-class times (from the child's entry into the building, to snack time, recess, the lunchroom, finding lockers, gym class, etc.) that prove to be the tipping points of success—or not—in general education or inclusive settings. The same level of thoughtfulness that goes into academic periods, goals, and interventions must be given to these situations. If a child has deficits in self-regulation, sensory, pragmatic language, or executive functioning and needs a consultant teacher or integrated co-teaching model to support them in math or ELA, it is extremely likely that these needs will be similar, if not exponential, during unstructured recess or a busy lunchroom. I don't understand when I see a child recommended for full-time ICT or have a 1:1 aide for classes who is then is left to recess or lunch with no plan or services.

Perhaps the most significant situation where these non-academic challenges come into play is in bullying. This issue is covered in more detail in Appendix E (page 211); any inclusive program or plan must have strong policies (and more importantly, actions) to fully monitor, address, and prevent these situations.

The child's level of needs and how they manifest interact in a complicated way with educational planning. There is something to be said about "the squeaky wheel" getting attention. This speaks to making sure that the "non-squeaky" aspects don't fall through the cracks. We often look for how proactive the team seems; their understanding that all aspects of the day can be critical opportunities for intervention or learning for a child. For example, a child on the spectrum who may isolate or do their own thing during free-play, and seems happy doing so, may not get the same level of attention as a child engaging in more outward behaviors.

A child's needs, even when they're in line with how a school system may understand them, can sometimes clash with programmatic or budgetary constraints. For instance, while a child may need a full-time integrated co-teaching environment (typically a full-time special education teacher who co-teaches with the general education teacher), the numbers of children in the grade may not allow for this. I have worked with many schools or districts that diligently try to make this work for the child by individualizing the program accordingly. This can be done by pushing-in the appropriate services and providers, such as: consultant teachers for instruction; occupational therapists for fine-motor or sensory supports; behaviorists to target behaviors; or speech and language pathologists for language support. Again, this must be individualized based on need. If the child truly needs full-time access to a special educator in the class, such as what could be delivered in an ICT class, alternative therapies need to be delivered at the same frequency.

Often programs delegate many responsibilities to aides or paraprofessionals. I have seen and worked with a full range of these support personnel and was even myself a paraprofessional in two schools prior to graduate school. I make no broad generalization that just because a person may not have an advanced degree that they cannot be effectual members of the team. I have been moved and impressed by many of these professionals across the years in certain contexts.

However, again, it is important to make sure the child's specific needs will be appropriately addressed. A child who has significant behavioral needs that warrant highly specialized active interventions will likely not be helped by simply having someone with them. At times, these poorly guided, albeit well-intentioned, personnel can exacerbate the difficulties. The level of training, supervision, staff development, and commitment of the special education team needs to be explored as it relates to aides and paraprofessionals.

We often query these areas to gauge the efficacy of the plan, which must clearly delineate the level of coordination expected between parents, the educational and therapy teams, and the aide. We have seen this range from school administration not allowing *any* correspondence between parents and aides to daily communication logs.

A general education or inclusive setting needs to be holistic to appropriately address the specific needs of a child. I've been so impressed with schools across the country and internationally that succeed with this approach. These schools integrate the child, not only in their classes but also actively programming unstructured times, such as social interventions delivered during lunch or recess, or in afterschool recreational programs.

When a child's needs are more intense and complex than can be met within an appropriate general education or inclusive classroom setting, a special education, self-contained class can be explored within a mainstream school. All too often decisions are dictated by what may be available given the numbers of children in the school at a given time.

There are many challenges to assuring the appropriateness of a self-contained class within a general education school. The extra challenge when the class is part of a larger community is how this is integrated and what is appropriate for the child. While it sounds good that placement in a special education class within a community school is more appropriate than a specialized school because it is less restrictive, this may only be true on paper. For some children, the access to typical peers may not be appropriate (or supported appropriately) for that child based on their presenting needs.

Investigating how that class or program is integrated into the school community, what supports are given to the child, and getting a sense of the overall culture of the school is imperative. Many programs do a good job of mixing the opportunities for more individualized instruction in areas needed, while providing appropriate supports during more inclusive periods of the day. However, some programs, either due to resources or structure, cannot appropriately meet the needs of all children within this model.

Looking at Self-Contained Classroom Settings

A good starting point is looking at the makeup of the class, ratio of support, and specialization of the interventions and instruction; this is true within a mainstream school or as part of a specialized or private special education school. These areas vary greatly across school systems. The child's needs, assessments, data gathered, and history should inform the level of interventions required, starting with the staffing ratio.

All too often I see IEP teams make a recommendation of a 12:1:1 or integrated class for a child transitioning from CPSE to CSE, despite clear indications and data on lack of progress and difficulties in their current, more restrictive, setting (like an 8:1:2 or full-time 1:1 SEIT support). If that child is not making appropriate progress with these intense supports in preschool, how could it be appropriate to take away interventions while increasing demands?

Self-contained classes range in size and ratios; the range, depth, and collaboration of the team of related service providers all need to be explored. Specialization and focus on the class does not always follow a definitive formula. Not all children on the autism spectrum must *only* be in a class for, and singularly focused on, ASD. However, given the specific needs of children on the spectrum, a high degree of specialization of the teacher and providers is often needed, and in many cases crucial.

"Special education" is not one-size-fits-all. The heterogeneity of the group and range of needs can help assess the appropriateness of the class and program. Some classes can have age ranges spanning 2–3 years and have children with a complete range of diagnoses, presentations, and needs. This is often quite difficult to negotiate and can make or break the child's success. We will often request a class makeup, including ages, classifications, and general cognitive and academic levels in order to assess the appropriateness. This is often the biggest challenge in making for an appropriate class.

Having a team that is part of the school and program being recommended can yield better potential recommendations and groupings. When a program is recommended as a general description and then handed over to others to find placement possibilities, much can be left to chance. More specialized private schools, where families apply and each child is assessed with consideration of the specific grouping, can have an advantage in this regard.

In assessing the appropriateness of a special education class for an individual child, we again look to see if the makeup of the class is set up to facilitate appropriate progress, social opportunities, and growth—or might the child's needs be too diluted, given the heterogeneity of presentations? We look to see the staff's level of training, levels of support personnel in the class, and the coordination and collaboration of the same.

Unfortunately, I have seen classes where any number of difficulties make for a concerning placement for a child. For example, classes with no clear behavioral structure or plan, despite the child's clear needs. Repeating a child's name over and over, or louder, is not a well-planned behavioral intervention: Behavioral management interventions should not be solely reactive. Children on the autism spectrum often need a comprehensive plan that is data-driven, analyzed, and implemented consistently. While this does not always speak to a full ABA program (nor does the scope of this chapter allow for fully addressing methodology), this level of service is often needed.

I believe that the core constructs of ABA are important, at least as a framework for making plans for many children on the autism spectrum. Whether the goals are increasing prosocial behaviors and functional communication or decreasing less adaptive behaviors, it is important to assess what motivates the child's behaviors to appropriately intervene. Different children can exhibit similar behaviors for completely different reasons, such as escape, avoiding attention, wanting attention or a tangible outcome, or being driven more internally by a sensory need. Interventions and teaching methods will be drastically different based on what is driving the behavior.

A good program in my opinion develops a well-established method of gathering and analyzing data; addressing and adjusting this plan actively; and fully coordinating among providers, teachers, aides, and family. I always look at how often data is gathered, what methods are used, and for clear knowledge by each staff member on the goals and targets of intervention for the child. This is even more critical with children who demonstrate greater needs in communication and behaviors. In brief, while different methodologies and philosophies exist, there should be appropriate flexibility and an individual needs assessment must be available and delivered. A program can call itself "eclectic" or pull from many intervention styles; at times this can indicate a lack of the specialization that may be needed as opposed to actually being armed with a range of interventions.

When a child exhibits more intensive behavioral issues, the plan and interventions need to match this level of need. If the child needs direct instruction from a BCBA, is this available? How often and in what contexts? For some children, an hour a day or group formats might be enough, for others those will not be sufficient. When I discuss "behavioral" issues, I do not only define this the way some systems define it. A child who is so self-directed that they do not participate in new challenges and constantly withdraws, yet is calm and quiet, is actually just as "behavioral" as a child who doesn't engage challenges but lashes out. Both children warrant a behaviorally informed approach to intervention. Does the school have the commitment to intervene at the same needed intensity? All of these factors are important in exploring special education classes within community schools or more restrictive settings.

Specialized Schools and Private Special Education Schools

There are instances when a general, inclusive education school setting cannot appropriately meet the level of individual needs presented by the child. In some cases, the "least restrictive" appropriate setting is a full-time special education school.

The efforts, methodology, and implementation of thoughtful and appropriate grouping is critical. This is imperative to secure the appropriate level of specialization and intervention—and to balance the appropriate level of modeling and peer opportunities. Often at IEP meetings, a team member will discuss the child's need for peer models, advocating for placement in a community school. What they may not appreciate is that, based on the child's needs, mainstream peers might be inappropriate for them; but an appropriately grouped special education class or school may have really good models or peers for them, even if they all have IEPs.

While specialized or private schools may possess greater resources or specialization for special education, that is not always paired with commensurate availability, collaboration, or flexibility in working with the child and their family. It goes without saying this is one of the most critical requisite needs for a school.

When a child warrants placement in a more specialized school based on deficits or weaknesses, the school's bandwidth must also properly address their strengths with opportunities for social, emotional, and academic growth and success. I have seen a full range of special education schools successfully thread this needle of providing intense supports while promoting and celebrating growth in other areas.

At times the complexity of a child's needs may require an even more restrictive educational plan. Programs that provide 1:1 direct instruction throughout the day (in a school, center, or home-based or alternative setting) may be warranted. These may be short-term or part of dual recommendations. Similarly, intensive program recommendations may include residential settings. As with all of the programs available, full assessment of the child's needs and the program's ability to address those needs must be fully vetted. These types of recommendations are not made lightly and should be actively monitored and reassessed.

Perhaps the most important general parameters lie in the transparency, sense of collaboration, and "team" approach between parents, professionals, and the school. I see it as my critical obligation as an evaluator to assist parents in the due diligence of exploring programs, which allows us to gather a general sense of how the school functions and a window into how they will be as partners. There are many extremely devoted, well-intentioned, and experienced professionals in the educational community and many wonderful programs. Yet, even with the best intentions, sometimes individual needs don't match the available resources or programs. Parents need to fully educate themselves, often with the help of experienced professionals, then ultimately trust their instincts and advocate accordingly.

Appendix C

Using Assessments and Evaluations to Develop a Reasonably Calculated and Appropriately Ambitious IEP[92]
By Dr. Jennifer Oratio, Ph.D.

A comprehensive evaluation that offers specific recommendations is an invaluable resource that can pave the way for positive changes in a child's life. In the context of developing a child's Individualized Education Plan (IEP), a comprehensive evaluation with specific recommendations can help shift the dialogue from "this is what loving parents want" to "this is what an informed professional is recommending." School districts (and judges) are especially receptive when a professional with no financial interest in the outcome is making the recommendation.[93]

The proper assessment of a child with special needs may initially seem like an overwhelming process. However, an informed parent can make choices to ensure a comprehensive evaluation that accurately pinpoints the child's strengths and challenges—and offers guidance to help the child make meaningful academic, developmental, and social-emotional gains.

Some families may already be acquainted with the array of evaluations traditionally provided by the local school district. However, parents may not be aware of a much more comprehensive evaluation, known as the "neuropsychological evaluation." Below are the key differences between evaluations and what they entail, as well as further expansion upon the types of professionals trained to administer them.

The neuropsychological evaluation is a comprehensive assessment administered by a clinician who has undergone specialized training as outlined in the Houston Conference Guidelines.[94] This individual is referred to as a Clinical Neuropsychologist, or when addressing children, a Pediatric or Child Neuropsychologist. They are specifically trained in brain-behavior relationships and in the application of assessment and intervention principles based on the study of human behavior across the lifespan, particularly as it pertains to normal and abnormal functioning of the central nervous system.

---

92 Parents regularly ask, "What are my child's rights?" The answer will be based on the answer to another, more fundamental question: "What are your child's unique needs?" The assessment process, when done right, should reveal those needs.

93 The assessment process will also help to identify and tease out the student's relative strengths. Accordingly, the evaluation process is essential to determining where to invest intervention resources efficiently.

94 **Houston Conference Guidelines**: Founded in 1997 by a select committee consisting of 37 Clinical Neuropsychologists, these guidelines provide a detailed description of an aspirational and integrated model of specialty education and training in clinical neuropsychology.

School Psychologists vs. Neuropsychologists
(Psychoeducational Evaluation vs. a Neuropsychological Evaluation)

At the school-district level, evaluations[95] are often administered by school psychologists. Rarely, however, are neuropsychologists employed by the local school district. School psychologists, unless they have undergone the specific training outlined by the Houston Conference Guidelines, are not authorized to present themselves as neuropsychologists. Only a neuropsychologist is qualified to engage in neuropsychological assessment.

A neuropsychological evaluation involves obtaining a comprehensive history of the student and undertaking a comprehensive record review. Observations are also important to provide meaningful qualitative information that complements the quantitative testing. Observations during testing are critical in further qualifying a student's performances; however, classroom observations are also important, as this allows the neuropsychologist to observe the student in natural surroundings.

Observing the student in school also lets examiner see firsthand if the student is well-adjusted in the classroom and whether the current placement is meeting his or her unique needs. When the classroom observation takes place prior to testing, it allows the examiner to have a vital "first look" to further design and determine an appropriate testing battery. It also prevents unnecessary distractions, feelings of self-consciousness, or anxiety that might occur if the student recognized the examiner/observer.

Testing appointments soon follow and, depending on the evaluator's preference, may involve multiple sessions lasting a total of six or more hours. The test battery is typically determined based on the "reason for referral" (the caregiver's current concerns). A typical neuropsychological testing battery consists of quantitative, standardized measures that evaluate a student's intellectual/cognitive skills (IQ), verbal and language abilities, nonverbal skills, memory skills, attention and executive functioning, academic functioning, social-emotional and behavioral functioning, and adaptive functioning.

Following these procedures, the neuropsychologist obtains and interprets the test results to determine what, if any, appropriate diagnoses are warranted and to give recommendations. A feedback session is then scheduled with the student's family to discuss the results of the evaluation. When appropriate, a separate session may also be scheduled with the student to provide a broad overview of strengths and weaknesses and introduce some techniques to improve areas of vulnerability. The feedback meeting is integral in discussing the findings and import of the evaluation and determine

---

95 Other than evaluations for OT, PT, or speech issues.

appropriate educational and treatment recommendations.

In marked contrast, a psychoeducational evaluation typically consists of cognitive assessments, academic testing, and a brief social-emotional-behavioral screen. At times, an adaptive measure may also be administered to a parent and/or teacher. The psychological evaluation does not explore any of the other above domains in depth and usually, at least when provided by a student's school district, does not provide diagnoses or recommendations for treatment. These matters are typically deferred to the school committee later when considering the development of an Individualized Education Program (IEP).

The goals and objectives of each type of evaluation may also be quite different. For instance, with an independent neuropsychological evaluation, specific referral concerns are thoroughly addressed and any appropriate diagnoses are assigned. Recommendations are highly specific and tailored to the neuropsychological findings and the student's needs; these are the end of the report, with the intention of effecting positive change. Notably, these recommendations are integral to program development and school placement—as well as securing necessary services, accommodations, and classroom modifications. Without them, the IEP team may be missing the basis for determining the type and frequency of services that the student might need.

An experienced neuropsychologist will carefully consider where the student is currently placed and will have reviewed the student's IEP (and other critical documents on the student's developmental, medical, psychiatric, and educational histories). Recommendations from this evaluation will also help determine if the current program is appropriate as-is, or if changes in placement or curriculum should occur. This changes the dynamic that typically is seen as "parent versus district" to "this is what the student needs."

Once the report is shared with the school district, it also is particularly useful to ask the neuropsychologist to participate in any upcoming meetings to discuss curriculum development or modification to a student's IEP to advocate for what the student requires per the findings of the evaluation. Conversely, if an evaluation (i.e., psychological or psychoeducational) is conducted by the district, the evaluator may not be permitted to make recommendations without the district's request or approval. This unhelpful roadblock minimizes the special expertise of the clinician and de-emphasizes program modification in favor of a "consensus" approach that can muddy the process or overlook what may be necessary for meaningful progress to take place.

Investing in a neuropsychological evaluation can be of great value to comprehensively evaluate a student's needs. However, because school districts typically do not provide these types of evaluations, families must seek them privately and pay for them out of pocket or, if they are fortunate, through insurance. You should be as informed as possible about your child's condition and unique needs. While paying out of pocket for a neuropsychological evaluation can be difficult for many families, its findings and recommendations can help to secure a child's future. The neuropsychological evaluation serves as a catalyst for change—something that is very difficult to put a price tag on.

Areas Assessed and Testing Measures

A neuropsychological evaluation examines many different areas of functioning and explores the brain-behavior relationship. Although neuropsychologists tend to use a core battery of tests depending on the referral question, they typically remain flexible and add or substitute certain measures to achieve the most accurate, useful information. Below are some of the most commonly used instruments for in a comprehensive neuropsychological evaluation, with further emphasis on those that should be incorporated when an autism diagnosis is in question.

Cognitive Assessment

Cognitive testing is a crucial first step in the neuropsychological evaluation process to better understand a student's strengths and weaknesses, during which the evaluator can uncover key patterns in how a student thinks and reasons. Among the most commonly used cognitive assessments are the Wechsler scales. Specifically, the Wechsler Intelligence Scale for Children, Fifth Edition®, or WISC-V ®[96], is an instrument designed for children ages 6–16 which measures intellectual skills across five major domain areas. Seven subtests comprise the full scale intelligence quotient (FSIQ); however, ancillary subtests can be administered to determine alternate indices and provide further information on strengths and weaknesses in verbal reasoning, verbal knowledge, visual-spatial skills, nonverbal reasoning, auditory and visual working memory, and processing speed.

The Wechsler Preschool and Primary Scale of Intelligence, Fourth Edition™ (WPPSI-IV™[97]) is also a measure that assesses cognitive functioning, but for children ages 2.5 through 7 years, 7 months. Like the WISC-V, the WPPSI-IV will calculate an FSIQ and offers

---

[96] Wechsler, D. (2014). Wechsler Intelligence Scale for Children (5th ed.) Bloomington, MN: NCS Pearson.
[97] Wechsler, D. (2012). Wechsler Preschool and Primary Scale of Intelligence (4th ed.) Bloomington, MN: NCS Pearson.

five Primary Index scales (i.e., Verbal Comprehension, Visual Spatial, Fluid Reasoning, Working Memory, and Processing Speed) and also includes several Ancillary Indices more specifically examine general ability, cognitive proficiency, nonverbal functioning, and vocabulary acquisition.

Another critical cognitive measure is the Stanford-Binet Intelligence Scales, Fifth Edition (SB-5[98]), an instrument that assesses intellectual abilities across the lifespan (2–85 years). It incorporates a full-scale IQ, verbal IQ, and nonverbal IQ tests, as well as well as five factor scores in each verbal and nonverbal domain that examine knowledge, visual-spatial skills, fluid reasoning, quantitative reasoning, and working memory.

As discussed, many cognitive assessments will provide a full-scale intelligence quotient (FSIQ), based on various task performances in specified areas that assess verbal and nonverbal functioning, as well as other areas of intellectual performance, such as cognitive proficiency skills. The FSIQ is a general estimate of cognitive ability but can at times underestimate intelligence and a student's potential to learn—especially with students who have uneven cognitive profiles or those who carry a diagnosis such as autism. When unevenness in performance occurs, the FSIQ is oftentimes rendered less useful or valid.

Therefore, to more accurately assess a student's intelligence with this type of profile, it is vital that each domain area be more closely and comprehensively examined. Some tests, such as the WISC-V ®, have derived supplemental indices for further interpretation of a student's level of functioning. An example of such a composite is the General Ability Index (GAI) of the WISC-V ®, which removes demands placed on higher-order cognitive processes such as working memory and processing speed; instead, it provides a general, more "pure" estimate of verbal and nonverbal intellectual functioning.

This composite can then be compared (or sometimes, contrasted) to the Cognitive Proficiency Index (CPI), which examines areas that are more influenced by executive functioning, attention and concentration, and mental efficiency. Drawing a comparison in these cases, in particular, can be particularly useful for students who have executive functioning vulnerabilities, which are frequently seen in the autism population. As mentioned, the WISC-V ® and other measures may also offer an ancillary Nonverbal Index, which focuses more exclusively on nonverbal skills.

---

98 Roid, G. H. (2003). Stanford-Binet Intelligence Scales (5th ed.) Itasca, IL: Riverside Pub.

Tests Measuring Nonverbal Intelligence

Tests of nonverbal intelligence also exist. For the purposes of these assessments, demands for verbal expression are removed and the load of processing and comprehending large amounts of language is limited. These options are especially important for evaluating students who are nonverbal or have difficulties with expressive communication—again, quite common presentations for those carrying a diagnosis on the autism spectrum.

The Test of Nonverbal Intelligence, Fourth Edition™ (TONI-4™[99]), is a language-free measure of cognitive functioning designed for individuals ages 6–90. Major areas measured are aptitude, abstract reasoning, problem solving, and intelligence. It also includes testing on items that contain one or more salient characteristics (i.e., shape, position, size, direction, rotation) that need to be analyzed and identified. Responses can be indicated through gestures such as pointing.

For younger children, the Primary Test of Nonverbal Intelligence (PTONI[100]) can be administered. The PTONI is designed for children ages 3 through 9 years, 11 months, and follows a similar format to the TONI-4™. Nonverbal reasoning abilities are assessed by having the student point to an item in a field of four that is different from the others. The Leiter International Performance Scale, Third Edition (Leiter-3[101]) is a completely nonverbal assessment of fluid intelligence serving individuals ages 3 years and older. Neither the examiner nor the examinee is required to speak and the test consists of game-like tasks with blocks. Attention, memory, and social-emotional rating scales are also included as a part of this measure.

Language-Based Assessments

It is especially important to include a formal language measure in the neuropsychological evaluation if the student has a history of language delay and subsequent difficulties with processing language, expressing thoughts through verbal communication, or utilizing language for social or functional adaptive purposes. In addition to information gathered from a student's history of language and communication and any associated delays, further language testing is frequently needed when there is an evident discrepancy on the cognitive measure between verbal and nonverbal functioning. Particular consideration should be given to those diagnosed on the autism spectrum, as difficulties with communication are inherent to the condition.

---

99   Brown, L., Sherbenou, R. J., & Johnsen, S. K. (2010). Test of Nonverbal Intelligence (4th ed.) Austin, TX: Pro-Ed.
100 Ehrler, D. J. & McGhee, R. L. (2008). Primary Test of Nonverbal Intelligence. Austin, TX: Pro-Ed.
101 Roid, G. H., Miller, L. J., Pomplun, N., & Koch, C. (2013). Leiter International Performance Scale (3rd ed.) Wood Dale, IL: Stoelting Co.

Instruments that evaluate language ability will typically provide an overall "core" language composite and performance capacity in specific areas of language, including receptive language and language comprehension skills, expressive language and knowledge of syntactic and grammatical rules, and pragmatic language and more sophisticated linguistic skills. Two common language assessments frequently administered by neuropsychologists are the Clinical Evaluation of Language Fundamentals, Fifth Edition® (CELF-5®[102]) and the Comprehensive Assessment of Spoken Language, Second Edition® (CASL-2®[103]). The CELF-5 ranges from ages 5–21 and specifically examines receptive and expressive language, language structure, and language content. The CASL-2® ranges from ages 3–21 and specifically assesses oral language, examining areas such as lexical and semantic knowledge, syntax, supralinguistic skills (those where language usage is more subtle, such as sarcasm), and pragmatic language.

For students who have more limited or delayed language, other measures may be more appropriate to administer. More specifically, picture vocabulary tests can provide useful information into verbal knowledge and vocabulary acquisition and can provide insight into the severity of delay.

The Receptive and Expressive One-Word Picture Vocabulary Tests, Fourth Edition (ROWPVT-4, EOWPVT-4[104]) are examples of such assessments and can compare receptive versus expressive vocabulary skills. On the ROWPVT-4, an individual matches a spoken word with an image of an object, action, or concept; on the EOWPVT-4, the student names, with one word, objects, actions, or concepts when presented with color illustrations. An overall composite score is derived for each assessment following administration. Similarly, the Peabody Picture Vocabulary Test, Fifth Edition™ (PPVT-5™[105]) is a measure designed to assess receptive vocabulary for individuals ages 2 ½ through 90-plus years and can provide useful information regarding language semantics and word knowledge.

Other neuropsychological measures, such as the NEPSY, Second Edition® (NEPSY®-II[106]), contain language domains that can provide additional useful information in areas

---

102 Semel, E., Wiig, E. H., & Secord, W. A. (2013). Clinical Evaluation of Language Fundamentals (5th ed.) Bloomington, MN: NCS Pearson.
103 Carrow-Woolfolk, E. (2017). Comprehensive Assessment of Spoken Language (2nd ed.) Torrance, CA: WPS.
104 Martin, N. A. & Brownell, R. B. (2010). Receptive and Expressive One-Word Picture Vocabulary Tests (4th ed.) Bloomington, MN: NCS Pearson.
105 Dunn, D. M. (2019-projected release date). Peabody Picture Vocabulary Test (5th ed.) Bloomington, MN: NCS Pearson.
106 Korkman, M., Kirk, U., & Kemp, S. (2007). NEPSY (2nd ed.) Bloomington, MN: NCS Pearson.

such as language comprehension, verbal fluency, and social pragmatics—in cases where language concerns are primary, administration of a specific language instrument may be warranted.

<u>Visual-Spatial and Visual-Motor Skills Assessment</u>

In some cases, it is necessary to further evaluate a student's nonverbal skills. Cognitive testing may indicate weaknesses in visual-spatial, visual-perceptual, visual-motor, and/or sensorimotor abilities that warrant administering more specific tests. Students with longstanding histories of motor skill development delays and weaknesses are particularly considered when administering such measures. Those who have required occupational or physical therapies, who have difficulty with motor coordination, or who have problems with graphomotor and the physical aspects of writing require further assessment in these specific areas. Specific testing may indicate conditions beyond what may be apparent (including diagnoses such as Developmental Coordination Disorder) or shed further light into a student's subcortical functioning and interrelated needs.

The Peabody Developmental Motor Scales, Second Edition (PDMS-2[107]) assesses motor skills in young children (i.e., birth through age 5 years) and focuses specifically on reflex response, stationary motor skills, locomotion, object manipulation, grasping, and visual-motor integration. Other measures that focus on visual-motor skills include the Beery-Buktenica Developmental Test of Visual-Motor Integration, Sixth Edition (BEERY™ VMI[108]), which looks at how well an individual can integrate visual and motor abilities. This measure can be administered to children as young as 2 years and also includes supplemental tasks that separately examine visual perception and motor coordination abilities. The NEPSY®-II also incorporates activities that assess developmental motor functioning in similar ways, such as the Design Copying, Visuomotor Precision, Imitating Hand Positions, and Manual Motor Sequences tasks.

Other measures, such as the Dean-Woodcock Neuropsychological Battery (DW[109]), can comprehensively evaluate sensorimotor functioning in greater depth at later ages as well (from age 4 through adulthood). The DW includes a Sensory-Motor Battery that consists of one measure of laterality, six sensory measures, and seven motor measures. The sensory measures examine peripheral and near point visual acuity, auditory acuity, and a variety of tactile functions; the motor tasks assess areas of gross motor functioning,

---

107   Folio, M. R. & Fewell, R. R. (2000). Peabody Developmental Motor Scales (2nd ed.) Torrance, CA: WPS.
108   Beery, K. E., Buktenica, N. A., & Beery, N. A. (2010). Beery-Buktenica Developmental Test of Visual-Motor Integration (6th ed.) Bloomington, MN: NCS Pearson.
109   Dean, R. S. & Woodcock, R. W. (2003). Dean-Woodcock Neuropsychological Battery. Itasca, IL: Houghton Mifflin Harcourt.

visual-motor construction, and coordination. Studies have shown this measure to be effective in for identifying important areas that need to be addressed across a broad spectrum of individuals, including those with autism and Attention-Deficit/Hyperactivity Disorder (ADHD).

Memory Assessment

Assessing memory is integral to understanding how a student processes different types of material and helps us understand how they best learn. Typically, measures that evaluate both verbal and visual memory are administered during a neuropsychological evaluation and are further broken down into contextualized and decontextualized tasks. Trials that provide recognition cuing should also be considered to determine if there is a problem with encoding material (i.e., the student never properly absorbed the material), or if there is difficulty with retrieval (i.e., the information has been processed, but the student has greater difficulty with accessing the learned information).

Common memory measures utilized by neuropsychologists include the Wide Range Assessment of Memory and Learning, Second Edition (WRAML-2[110]); the Children's Memory Scale® (CMS[111]); and the California Verbal Learning Test®, Children's Edition (CVLT®-C[112]). The WRAML-2 provides a number of verbal memory, visual memory, as well as attention and concentration tasks that tap into executive functioning areas such as working memory. The verbal and visual measures can examine both immediate recall and delayed recall; assesses an individual's memory for information presented in context (i.e., stories, familiar scenes) and out of context (i.e., word lists, abstract designs); and many also include recognition trials to determine if cuing assists in further recall.

The CMS has a similar format, with tasks that assess verbal and visual memory during short- and long-term trials; examine both recall and recognition; and includes activities that tap into attention and working memory. The CVLT®-C measures multi-trial learning and long-term recall abilities, strictly for verbal information. Supplemental trials include an interference list, short-delay free and cued recall, long-delay free and cued recall, and recognition. In addition to these measurements, specific memory tasks from the NEPSY-II® can be administered to examine verbal and visual memory delivered in context (i.e., Narrative Memory, Sentence Repetition, Memory for Names, Memory for Faces) and out of context (i.e., List Memory, Word List Interference, Memory for Designs).

---

[110] Sheslow, D., & Adams, W. (2003). Wide Range Assessment of Memory and Learning (2nd ed.) Lutz, FL: PAR Inc.

[111] Cohen, M. (1997). Children's Memory Scale. Bloomington, MN: The Psychological Corporation.

[112] Delis, D. C., Kramer, J. H., Kaplan, E., & Ober, B. A. (1994). California Verbal Learning Test – Children's Version. Bloomington, MN: The Psychological Corporation.

Assessing Executive Function Deficits

Executive functioning essentially refers to an individual's system of self-governance, self-monitoring, and self-regulation. It provides us with the ability to organize, plan, initiate and maintain activity, learn from past mistakes, and change our behavior to conform to environmental demands. Current models of self-regulation suggest that behavioral and emotional regulation also underlie most other areas of executive functioning. Essentially, one needs to be appropriately inhibited, flexible, and under emotional control for efficient, systematic, and organized problem solving to take place.

Measures that assess executive functioning will include tasks that tap metacognitive skills such as attention, concentration, working memory, processing speed, planning, organization, cognitive flexibility, self-initiation, and self-monitoring. It also addresses behavioral and emotional regulation ability, emotional control, inhibition skills, and behavioral shifting. Typically, a mix of quantitative tests and behavior rating scales are administered during the neuropsychological evaluation. Rating scales may be completed by parents, caregivers, teachers, and other instructors or staff. Self-report versions are also available for students who are old enough and have enough insight into their functioning in these areas. Students with a history of attention problems, those diagnosed with ADHD, or those who have exhibited increased difficulty with these skills (including many individuals on the autism spectrum) should be especially considered for comprehensive assessment into this area.

Quantitative measures that examine a student's level of executive functioning typically assess areas such as planning and organization, cognitive flexibility and inhibitory control, fluency skills, self-regulation, and sustained attention. Instruments commonly utilized during the administration of a neuropsychological evaluation are the Delis-Kaplan Executive Function System™ (D-KEFS™[113]), designed for individuals from age 8– 89 years or tasks from the NEPSY-II® (i.e., Statue, Animal Sorting, Auditory Attention and Response Set, Inhibition) for ages 3–16 years. Supplemental measures can also be utilized in conjunction with these tests, including the Wisconsin Card Sorting Test®[114], designed for ages 6 years, 5 months through 89 years to examine specific abilities in strategic planning, organized searching, cognitive shifting, self-regulation, and problem-solving.

Sustained attention tasks are also very useful in measuring attentional control.

---

[113] Delis, D. C., Kaplan, E., & Kramer, J. H. (2001). Delis-Kaplan Executive Function System. Bloomington, MN: NCS Pearson.

[114] Grant, D. A. & Berg, E. A. (1981). Wisconsin Card Sorting Test. Torrance, CA: WPS.

The Conners Continuous Performance Test, 3rd Edition™ (Conners CPT 3™[115]) is a computerized visual assessment designed for children 8 years and older that examines performance in areas such as sustained attention, inattention, impulsivity, and vigilance. The CPT 3 can be used in conjunction with the Conners Continuous Auditory Test of Attention™ (Conners CATA™[116]), which assesses auditory processing and attention. For younger students (i.e., those ages 4–7 years), the Conners Kiddie Continuous Performance Test, Second Edition (K-CPT 2[117]) is available. The Test of Variables of Attention (T.O.V.A.®), Version 9[118], is a separate continuous performance task for individuals ages 4 years and older and measures integral components of attention and inhibitory control in response to auditory or visual stimuli.

In addition to quantitative tests administered to a student during the neuropsychological evaluation, it is important to gauge the level of functioning in this area across other settings. Behavior rating scales can provide valuable insights into a student's skills outside of the testing office, such as at home and at school. One of such types of assessment tools is the Behavior Rating Inventory of Executive Function®, Second Edition (BRIEF®2[119]), used for students between 5–18 years. Parent, teacher, and self-report questionnaires are available that examine areas that encompass inhibitory self-control, flexibility, and metacognition.

The Conners 3rd Edition™ (Conners 3®[120]) is a separate, thorough assessment for students between 6–18 years that examines attention and executive functioning, specifically pertaining to diagnoses of ADHD and comorbid conditions. Rating forms are available for parents, caregivers, teachers, and students. Similarly, the Vanderbilt ADHD Diagnostic Rating Scale (VADRS)[121] and Swanson, Nolan, and Pelham Questionnaire, Fourth Edition (SNAP-IV, Teacher and Parent Rating Scale)[122] assess symptoms that are related to ADHD criteria and related externalizing and internalizing conditions; these are completed by the student's parent/caregiver and teacher. The VADRS is designed to assess ADHD-related symptoms for children ages 6–12 years and the SNAP-IV ranges

---

115   Conners, C. K. (2014). Conners Continuous Performance Test (3rd ed.) Toronto, ON: MHS Assessments.
116   Conners, C. K. (2014). Conners Continuous Auditory Test of Attention. Toronto, ON: MHS Assessments.
117   Conners, C. K. (2015). Conners Kiddie Continuous Performance Test (2nd ed.) Toronto, ON: MHS Assessments.
118   Greenberg, L. M., Holder, C., Kindschi, C. L., Dupuy, T. R., & Hughes, S. J. (2017). Test of Variables of Attention (9th ed.) Los Alamitos, CA: The TOVA Company.
119   Gioia, G. A., Isquith, P. K., Guy, S. C., & Kenworthy, L. (2015). Behavior Rating Inventory of Executive Function (2nd ed.) Lutz, FL: PAR Inc.
120   Conners, C. K. (2008). Conners (2nd ed.) Toronto, ON: MHS Assessments.
121   Wolraich, M. (2002) Vanderbilt ADHD Diagnostic Rating Scale.
122   Swanson, J. M., Nolan, E., & Pelham, W. (1983) Swanson, Nolan, and Pelham Questionnaire.

from ages 6–18 years.

Assessing Academic Achievement

Although academic functioning is assessed in both psychoeducational and neuropsychological evaluations, typically more in-depth educational testing is administered during the more comprehensive neuropsychological evaluation. In addition to broad academic assessment, in some cases (i.e. when investigating the presence of a specific learning disorder), it is necessary to further delineate levels of functioning in more specific areas by administering measures with a more concentrated focus in evaluating such skills.

The Wechsler Individual Achievement Test®, Third Edition (WIAT®-III[123]) is a nationally standardized measure of academic achievement designed for students in pre-kindergarten through 12th grade that assesses skills in reading (i.e., sight word reading, decoding, comprehension, and fluency); written expression (i.e., spelling, compositional ability); and mathematics (calculations, applied math, math fluency); as well as areas such as listening comprehension and oral expression.

The Woodcock-Johnson® IV Tests of Achievement (WJ-IV[124]) is another nationally normed academic achievement test for students in pre-kindergarten through 12th grade that measures four broad academic domains: reading, written language, mathematics, and academic knowledge. Similarly, the Kaufman Test of Educational Achievement, Third Edition (KTEA™-3[125]), designed for grades pre-kindergarten through 12, assesses key academic skills in reading, math, written language, and oral language. Patterns of strength and weakness can be derived from each of these measures to determine any potential learning disabilities and inform decisions regarding eligibility for educational services and/or placement.

As mentioned, more specific assessments may be necessary to properly delineate the presence of a learning disability. For example, when a specific learning disorder with impairment in reading is suspected, additional measures such as the Gray Oral Reading Test, Fifth Edition (GORT-5[126]) should be considered in conjunction with the measures discussed above. The GORT-5 is designed for students ages 6–24 years and requires a student to read various passages aloud, then respond to orally presented comprehension questions. This measure is successful in identifying students performing

---

123 Wechsler, D. (2009). Wechsler Individual Achievement Test (3rd ed.) Bloomington, MN: NCS Pearson.
124 Schrank, F. A., McGrew, K. S., & Mather, N. (2014). Woodcock-Johnson (4th ed.) Rolling Meadows, IL: Riverside.
125 Kaufman, A. S. & Kaufman, N. L. (2014). Kaufman Test of Educational Achievement (3rd ed.) Bloomington, MN: NCS Pearson.
126 Wiederholt, J. L. & Bryant, B. R. (2012). Gray Oral Reading Test (5th ed.) Austin, TX: Pro-Ed.

significantly below their peers in oral reading proficiency and provides performance scores in the areas of reading accuracy, reading rate, reading fluency, and reading comprehension.

For further assessment of writing, the Test of Written Language, Fourth Edition (TOWL-4[127]) may be administered. This measure ranges from ages 9–18 years and examines vocabulary, spelling, punctuation, sentence composition and combining, and story composition skills. The KeyMath™-3 Diagnostic Assessment[128] ranges from kindergarten through 12th grade and comprehensively measures essential math concepts and skills spanning conceptual knowledge, computational skills, and problem solving (i.e., numeration, algebra, geometry, measurement, data analysis and probability, operations, mental computation and estimation, written computation, applied problem solving). Assessing these areas can pinpoint even more specific strengths and weaknesses, can identify if a specific learning disorder in math is present, and can better assist in academic remediation planning.

Social/Emotional/Behavioral Assessment

Measures that assess social-emotional and behavioral functioning range from broad screening scales to questionnaires that are quite specific to different conditions. While there are a number of these types of assessments, below are some of the more common measures used.

The Behavior Assessment System for Children, Third Edition (BASC-3[129]) is a multidimensional rating scale that assesses children from preschool age through early adulthood. Parent, teacher, and self-report questionnaires are available that screen for symptoms of internalizing (i.e., depression, anxiety); externalizing/behavioral (oppositional behavior, aggression, conduct problems); social; and those related to developmental/adaptive issues. Results indicate developing and immediate issues of concern and suggest possible diagnoses associated with areas identified as problematic.

Results from this measure can also be used to assist in behavior intervention plans (BIPs), as well as recommendations for services for IEPs. The Conners Comprehensive Behavior Rating Scales™ (Conners CBRS®[130]) is another multi-informant assessment of children and adolescents that spans ages 6–18. It assesses for a variety of behaviors, emotional symptoms, and academic and social problems across settings and can better

---

[127] Hammill, D. D. & Larsen, S. C. (2009). Test of Written Language (4th ed.) Austin, TX: Pro-Ed.
[128] Connolly, A. J. (2007). KeyMath Diagnostic Assessment (3rd ed.) San Antonio, TX: Pearson.
[129] Reynolds, C. R. & Kamphaus, R. W. (2015). Behavior Assessment System for Children (3rd ed.) Bloomington, MN: NCS Pearson.
[130] Conners, C. K. (2008). Conners Comprehensive Behavior Rating Scales. Toronto, ON: MHS Assessments.

inform potential diagnoses, as well as assist in educational and treatment planning.

When students are struggling in particular areas—academic, social, emotional, or behavioral—it may be useful to investigate their current level of self-esteem, as this information can help identifying issues that require treatment or that need to be addressed. The Piers-Harris™ Self-Concept Scale, Third Edition (Piers-Harris™ 3)[131] is a self-report measure for individuals ages 6–22 that provides a complete picture of self-concept and provides information regarding behavioral adjustment, freedom from anxiety and dysphoric mood states, happiness and life satisfaction, intellectual ability and school status, physical appearance and body image, and social acceptance. Results from this measure can help to guide appropriate treatment planning and support students in specific ways across settings.

After these screening measures have been administered, more comprehensive assessment into specific diagnoses may be warranted depending on the presenting issues. Since anxiety can accompany many other conditions in children (including ASD, ADHD, and Specific Learning Disorders), more in-depth examination may be needed, particularly if certain scales are elevated. Record review and/or qualitative interviews with parents, students, and other providers could also indicate this as an area of concern.

The Multidimensional Anxiety Scale for Children, Second Edition™ (MASC-2™[132]) is a comprehensive multi-rater assessment of anxiety in children and adolescents ages 8–19 years. It distinguishes between dimensions and types of anxiety and indexes a severity of overall anxiety symptoms. A separate rating inventory that assesses for depressive symptoms in children and adolescents (ages 7–17) is the Children's Depression Inventory 2nd Edition™ (CDI 2®[133]). Key areas examined are emotional problems such as negative mood, physical symptoms, and negative self-esteem and functional problems, including interpersonal problems and feelings of ineffectiveness. An overall total score is confirms the likelihood that a depressive condition exists and better informs treatment recommendations.

<u>Evaluating Adaptive Skills</u>

Adaptive behavior scales examine functional skills necessary for daily living across settings. These rating scales are typically designed for parents/caregivers, as well as teachers and service providers within the school environment. Two measures typically

---

131 Viers, E. V. & Herzberg, D. S. (2002). Piers-Harris (3rd ed.) Torrance, CA: WPS.
132 March, J. S. (2012). Multidimensional Anxiety Scale for Children (2nd ed.) Toronto, ON: MHS Assessments.
133 Kovacs, M. (2010). Children's Depression Inventory (2nd ed.) Toronto, ON: MHS Assessments.

utilized by evaluators are the Vineland Adaptive Behavior Scales, Third Edition (Vineland-3)[134] and the Adaptive Behavior Assessment System, Third Edition (ABAS-3).[135] Both measures evaluate children, adolescents, and adults from birth through age 90 and provide an overall adaptive composite that can assist in diagnosing, as well as help determine eligibility for important services within and outside the school setting. The Vineland-3 assesses adaptive skills that fall into three major domains: communication, daily living skills, and socialization. Other supplemental indices are available, but optional (i.e., Motor Skills and Maladaptive Behavior). The ABAS-3 is split into three major domains assessing conceptual, social, and practical skills. Strengths and weaknesses in each of these areas can be determined to aid in program development.

Autism-Specific Assessments

When there is a question of an autism diagnosis, it is essential that the examiner utilizes specific instruments that can properly differentiate this condition from others. Most often, these assessment measures are administered by a neuropsychologist or other trained professional upon first diagnosis; some can also provide useful information after a diagnosis has already been assigned (i.e., determining if severity level has increased or decreased). Below, several of the most important autism screening and assessment measures are discussed.

Widely considered the "gold standard" in assessing the existence of an autism diagnosis, the Autism Diagnostic Observation Schedule™, Second Edition (ADOS™-2)[136] is a semi-structured, standardized assessment of communication, social interaction, play, and restricted and repetitive behaviors. These areas are assessed via observation by highly trained clinical or research professionals. Behaviors and the quality of interactions with the student are coded during specific social "presses" or social interaction opportunities and that coding later informs the presence and severity level of an ASD diagnosis.

Examples of social situations during testing include those that tap for joint attention, social reciprocity, imitation skills, social communication, emotional awareness and expression, and social initiation. There are five modules that comprise the ADOS™-2, including a toddler module for young children between 12–30 months who do not consistently use phrase speech. The other four modules are based primarily on developmental language level; only one module is administered at the time of

---

134 Sparrow, S. S., Cicchetti, D. V. & Saulnier, C. A. (2016). Vineland Adaptive Behavior Scales (3rd ed.) Bloomington, MN: NCS Pearson.
135 Harrison, P. & Oakland, T. (2015). Adaptive Behavior Assessment System (3rd ed.) Torrance, CA: WPS.
136 Lord, C. & Rutter, M. (2012). Autism Diagnostic Observation Schedule (2nd ed.) Torrance, CA: WPS.

evaluation.

The Autism Diagnostic Interview™, Revised (ADI™-R)[137] is a comprehensive structured interview that takes place between the clinician and the parent/caregiver designed to assess for the presence of autism. The ADI™-R takes 1.5–2.5 hours to administer and frequently accompanies the administration of the ADOS™-2. The ADI™-R focuses on three major domains: language and communication skills, reciprocal social interaction ability, and repetitive/stereotyped behaviors and interests. Administration of this measure can further support a diagnosis of autism or differentiate it from other developmental conditions and can help determine the clinical needs of the individual.

Other, more brief screening measures for ASD can also be administered as part of the neuropsychological evaluation. One of these measures is the Childhood Autism Rating Scale™, Second Edition (CARS™-2[138]). This measure assesses for symptoms of autism in children ages 2 years and older and consists of both parent/caregiver and clinician rating scales. For the clinician rating scale, either a Standard Version or High Functioning Version is chosen; the latter is indicated for individuals who are more verbally fluent, 6 years or older, and have at least Low Average IQs.

Functional areas assessed on these scales include relating to people, imitation skills, social understanding, emotional response, emotional expression and regulation of emotions, body use, object use in play, adaptation to change, visual response, listening response, taste/smell/touch response and use, fear/anxiety, verbal communication, nonverbal communication, activity level, thinking and cognitive integration skills, level and consistency of intellectual response, and overall clinician impressions. Rating values of all items are added to produce a total score that indicates the presence and severity level of autism.

Similarly, the Gilliam Autism Rating Scale, Third Edition (GARS-3)[139] spans ages 3–22 and is a frequency-based rating scale that can be completed by parents, teachers, or clinicians and is used to assist in diagnosis of an ASD and to estimate its severity. The Social Communication Questionnaire (SCQ)[140] is another brief instrument that evaluates communication and social functioning in those who may present with autism. Content areas parallel those of the ADI™-R, and results can be used to guide treatment and educational planning.

---

[137] Rutter, M. & Lecouteur, A. (2003). Autism Diagnostic Interview, Revised. Torrance, CA: WPS.
[138] Schopler, E., Van Bourgondien, M. E., Wellman, G. J. & Love, S. R. (2010). Childhood Autism Rating Scale (2nd ed.) Torrance, CA: WPS.
[139] Gilliam, J. E. (2013). Gilliam Autism Rating Scale (3rd ed.) Austin, TX: Pro-Ed.
[140] Rutter, M., Bailey, A. & Lord, C. (2003). Social Communication Questionnaire. Torrance, CA: WPS.

Like the three aforementioned rating scales, the Social Responsiveness Scale™, Second Edition (SRS™-2)[141] is a questionnaire designed to screen for the presence of ASD and ranges from age 2.5 years through adulthood; both parent and teacher forms are available to assess symptomatology across home and school settings. A total score that reflects severity of symptoms related to ASD is calculated, along with five subscales (i.e., social awareness, social cognition, social communication, social motivation, and restricted interests and repetitive behavior) that can be helpful for designing treatment programs.

Although the Assessment of Basic Language and Learning Skills, Revised (ABLLS-R)[142] is not a measure typically administered by a neuropsychologist, it is an important and useful instrument that may be used by a student's school or therapy instructor. The ABLLS-R is based on the principles of Verbal Behavior[143] and serves as a tool to assess the baseline of language, academic, motor, social, and self-help skills of children with autism and other developmental disabilities. A tailored language-based curriculum is then created, with goals specific to each identified area. Skills are thereafter tracked to monitor progress in each domain.

The Verbal Behavior Milestones Assessment and Placement Program (VB-MAPP)[144] is a similar type of assessment that is also based upon Verbal Behavior principles and focuses on language, learning, and social development. It is a criterion-referenced tool that provides a baseline assessment prior to intervention, identifies developmentally appropriate targets for intervention, develops a skills training program. VB-MAPP also allows opportunities for follow-up assessment to determine progress in specific skill areas, as well as existing areas of deficits and strengths. If an ABLLS-R or VB-MAPP have been completed and is in use for the student, the neuropsychologist will likely want to examine the results, see what type of curriculum has been developed, and incorporate this information into the neuropsychological report.

Sharing Evaluations with the School District

Following testing, a feedback session is coordinated with the student's family (and with the student, if appropriate). However, communication of evaluation findings should

---

141 Constantino, J. N. (2012). Social Responsiveness Scale (2nd ed.) Torrance, CA: WPS.
142 Partington, J. W. (2006). Assessment of Basic Language and Learning Skills, Revised. Pleasant Hill, CA: Partington Behavior Analysts.
143 **Verbal Behavior** is a term first coined by behaviorist B.F. Skinner in 1957 to describe a behavioral approach to the acquisition of language. Teaching based upon these principles has been developed to increase communication skills.
144 Sundberg, M. L. (2008). Verbal Behavior Milestones Assessment and Placement Program. Concord, CA: AVB Press.

not end there. Except in unusual circumstances, the neuropsychological evaluation report is important information that should be shared with the student's school district and its team of professionals, including teachers, related service providers (i.e., speech therapists, occupational therapists, school counselors), principals/assistant principals, and district representatives. In most cases, the neuropsychological evaluation report should speak for itself, but it can be exponentially more helpful for the neuropsychologist to participate in consultation and meetings (i.e., IEP meetings) with the school and/or district to explain and clarify areas of the evaluation report—as well as advocate for the recommendations in the report.

Follow-Up Assessment and Measuring Progress

Finally, it is important to follow up with re-assessment to determine the level of progress made since recommendations were made and interventions introduced into the student's program. Whereas some of the aforementioned measures (i.e., ABLLS, VB-MAPP) will track progress through its own systems, other measures need to be re-administered by the neuropsychologist and then statistically compared to calculate measurable progress.

The reliable change index (RCI)[145] is an example of such a procedure that can inform where a student has made statistical gains or still needs ongoing, increased, or different types of support. The neuropsychologist can calculate the RCI for any number of tests deemed useful in addressing pertinent issues related to the student's developmental, learning, and/or social-emotional needs. In turn, this information can be included in a re-evaluation report to discuss the student's response to intervention and to determine any updates or changes in programming that need to occur. Over time, with appropriate, comprehensive evaluations and the introduction of appropriate intervention and evolution of programming, we should see meaningful progress made—as well as a "gap" or disparity amongst skill sets diminishing.

---

145 The **Reliable Change Index (RCI)** is a statistic that assesses whether a change in an individual's score (e.g. before and after some intervention) is statistically significant or not. It is defined as the change in a score divided by the standard error of the difference for the test being used.

Appendix D

Evaluating Speech and Language Needs with the Right Assessment Tools
By Dr. Steven Blaustein, CCC-SLP

If your child has been diagnosed on the autism spectrum, a comprehensive speech and language assessment conducted by a certified speech-language pathologist—one who is highly experienced and skilled in the evaluation and treatment of individuals with autism is essential to ascertain your child's communication level, determine the range of interventions that are warranted, and provide evidence-based support to assist in the development of an appropriate IEP.

Having a wide range of experience with different assessment tools is important. It is equally important, however, to select a professional who understands and can recommend specific interventions, determine the frequency and durations of therapies, complete a clear and well-written diagnostic report, and is knowledgeable about available sources of service delivery.

A speech-language pathologist must also be available, if needed, to advocate for the services needed. That advocacy may be required at IEP meetings, impartial hearings, phone calls with insurance companies, or discussions with school personnel (most often to answer questions regarding the evaluation and/or the child's unique communication needs).

The evaluator also must be familiar with the latest evidence-based approaches to assessment and interventions for ASD; local, state and federal statutes, regulations, and guidelines impacting provision of services; and be experienced working interprofessionally. The speech-language pathologist must be able to interpret progress notes, school reports, and related evaluations from psychologists, neurologists, developmental pediatricians, ABA providers, teachers, etc.

The speech-language pathologist needs to be able to appreciate the "big picture" by incorporating information gleaned from the reports of other professionals to present a cohesive, collaborative, and clear picture of the individual being assessed.

Speech-language pathologists must be licensed by the state in which they practice and should hold a Certificate of Clinical Competence (CCC) from the American Speech Language and Hearing Association (ASHA).

To conceptualize how communication is assessed for an individual, it is helpful to understand the multiple sub-areas of communication that must be evaluated. A thorough evaluation should consist of the reason for referral, relevant background information, behavioral observations across settings, standardized norm-referenced professionally recognized tests, informal assessments (also referred to as authentic assessment), and an evaluation of the oral-peripheral articulators. The exact nature, length, number of tests, and time spent will vary based on the level, abilities, and age of the individual being assessed.

The observation section is a critical part of any speech and language evaluation. It is an informal assessment of the individual's behaviors during the evaluation that affect communication, test performance and the individual's ability to cooperate, and participate and respond under varying conditions.

An important part of this section is the issue of the student's attention. The evaluator should look for the ability to engage in joint attention, sustained attention during tasks, and the ability to transition between tasks, reengage, and maintain attention. Elements such as relatedness, distractibility, consistency of response, activity level, and any additional behaviors affecting an individual's performance during the assessment will be noted, as they positively or negatively impact the assessment and might possibility impact future individual or group therapy or a classroom setting. These areas of attention are largely mediated by executive function, a critical area of development that allows us to learn, organize, and effectively use information. An assessment of these areas would also be noted in a psychological or neurological report.

Speech sound *production* must also be assessed. Commonly known as "pronunciation or articulation," this refers to the ability to produce and sequence the sounds of our language that enable an individual to learn and eventually produce clear, intelligible, functional language. It is the ability to make precise, rapid, dynamic movements of the lips, tongue, jaw, and velum (soft palate) that acoustically result in the "sounds" necessary to produce language.

The speech-language pathologist will assess "articulation" through standardized, norm-referenced instruments such as the Arizona-4 or Goldman-Fristoe Test of Articulation. These assessments will allow the evaluator to reliably determine the individual's functional level of speech sound development. Informal assessment of speech sound production is done during play, other informal activities, or tasks where the evaluator will make a determination on the overall intelligibility of speech during informal language use. Additional targeted, specific assessment instruments may be used if difficulties with speech sound production are suspected.

Apraxia signifies difficulty with speech sound production, something that is quite common in children diagnosed with ASD. Apraxia results in difficulty organizing and "motor planning" the speech sounds in the correct order. Dysarthria, on the other hand, is a peripheral weakness of the articulators and is attributed to possible neurological difficulty. Speech sounds may also be "delayed" where a child is acquiring the sounds of the language but at a slower rate than expected. These possible difficulties with speech sound production must be ruled out, evaluated, reliably diagnosed, and explained; specific skilled interventions and therapeutic approaches should be recommended if necessary.

As part of the speech evaluation assessment, the "oral peripheral" articulators should be assessed. This is an evaluation of the structure and function of the "articulators" or parts of the mouth that are responsible for producing the speech sounds.

The jaw, teeth, tongue, hard and soft palates, and pharynx will be examined to determine that they are intact with no structural anomalies to interfere with speech production. A shortened lingual frenulum (tongue tie) may restrict movement of the tongue and interfere with certain consonant productions that require anterior tongue movement. An individual's occlusion or bite may have an impact on speech production, as will missing teeth. The "function" of the articulators refers to how they move. The ability to imitate movements of the articulators include pursing and retracting the lips (puckering and smiling) and extending and lateralizing the tongue. Difficulty with movement of the articulators may also negatively impact speech sound production. Rapid alternating movements of the articulators are assessed through timing rapid productions of speech sounds such as "papapa," "tatata" or "pataka." This is known as diadochokinetic rate. There are age-expected speeds of repetition that are used to determine an individual's ability. A slow rate may affect timing of speech while difficulty sequencing the sounds may be indicative of a speech sound disorder such as apraxia (correct sequencing of sounds).

The speech pathologist should also assess sensory responses in and around the mouth. Children with ASD may have oromotor tactile "defensiveness" and not like being touched in the oral area. This could impact speech therapy aimed at speech sound production and there are specific interventions to assist in this area. Swallowing, eating, and drinking may also be assessed. It is not uncommon for children with ASD to have limited diets and present with sensory textural, flavor, or consistency aversions that impact eating. These areas must be evaluated to determine if additional interventions are necessary as part of the IEP.

Language is a critical and essential area of communication that must be thoroughly and adequately assessed. Language is the core of how one communicates, shares thoughts and emotions, expresses needs, and enables others to understand them as individuals. Language acquisition begins at birth and develops throughout the lifespan.

The assessment of language must consider the age of the individual, expected typical competencies for their age, performance level of the individual being assessed, and barriers to expected levels. A diagnosis of ASD will present challenges and barriers to many, if not all, areas of language that are assessed. Delineating specific areas of language strengths and weaknesses, specifying levels of function, understanding their impact on communication, and documenting these results are essential to a proper diagnosis—and ultimately, to proper intervention.

Language may be broadly conceptualized into receptive language (comprehension), expressive language (what we say), and pragmatics (functional and social use of language). Given the various areas of language to be assessed, the discrete sub-skills that make up language, and considering the age and skill level of the individual, careful attention must be given to selecting standardized tests. This selection process should consider which assessment tools will produce the most appropriate data that will specify the individual's functional level, help explain language performance, guide intervention targets, and aid in making recommendations. Standardized assessments begin at younger than 3 months and are available for ages through 21 years to adult. Thus, the examiner must be fully aware of the variety, nature, reliability, and validity of available test materials to select the appropriate test battery.

Overall language comprehension and expression must also be thoroughly assessed, evaluating what the individual understands. Relevant sub-skills in this area include (but are not limited to): vocabulary, grammar, sentence structure, paragraph-level language, stories, following directions, answering questions, and an overall evaluation of language processing.

Popular assessment instruments for this type of testing include the Clinical Evaluation of Language Fundamentals-Preschool 2 (3–6 years); Clinical Evaluation of Language Fundamentals-5 (5 years to 21 years 11 months); Comprehensive Assessment of Spoken Language-2 (3–21 years). Other tests with subtle differences are available and should be considered depending upon the level and age of the client. Once a general assessment of comprehension is completed, there may be indication of weaknesses in other specific areas.

Phonological awareness is a child's knowledge of how sounds work and is an important requisite to reading. The Comprehensive Test of Phonological Processing (CTOPP-2) may be used to assess this area. If weaknesses are suspected in memory, a test such as the Token Test for Children or the Test of Auditory Processing Skills-4 may be administered, which assesses aspects of phonological awareness; memory for numbers, words, and sentences; memory for digits in reverse order; and aspects of understanding directions and language comprehension. Many other tests can be considered.

Expressive language consists of what an individual is able to say and the way words are put together to form phrases, sentences, and stories. Again, if difficulty or weakness is suspected based on the more general test administered, there is a large array of specific, specialized tests that can be administered to further assess expressive language. This can include tests of single-item expressive vocabulary such as the Expressive One-Word Picture Vocabulary Test-4 or Expressive Vocabulary Test-2. The ability to tell stories at different levels may be assessed via the Test of Narrative Language-2 and subtests of the Test of Language Development-Intermediate or Test of Adolescent and Adult Language.

Pragmatic language is a difficult area to assess. Pragmatics is the way we use language; our intent or purpose; and the numerous ways language can be used, such as to comment, question, request, negate, etc. Pragmatics is also a much broader umbrella term covering the "rules" of language, including: recognizing listener needs, maintaining conversational turns and topics, initiating language, being a respondent, providing contingent responses to questions and comments, reading body language and facial expressions, and being a functional, competent language user. A primary weakness for individuals with a diagnosis of Autism Spectrum Disorder is in this area of pragmatic language; it therefore needs to be carefully and thoroughly assessed so that proper intervention strategies and recommendations can be made. The acquisition of pragmatic language is essential to promote greater levels of independence.

Reliably assessing pragmatic language skills via standardized testing is a controversial topic. There are standardized assessment instruments such as the Test of Pragmatic Language Skills, subtests on pragmatics from the Test of Integrated Language and Literacy, and related tests such as Test of Problem Solving that are recommended to formally assess pragmatic language in a standardized manner. Given the dynamic nature of language use—and the rapid, ongoing demands that change with speaking situations, the individual to whom one is speaking, individual or group situations, the environment, and many other considerations—it is impossible to reliably assess this extremely complex area with a formal test. Informal assessments by a highly skilled and experienced speech-language pathologist must be completed across a variety of settings. Parent, teacher, and service provider reports and observations must be considered as well. Results will determine which intervention strategies are needed, including opportunities for typical peer modeling or pragmatic social skills groups.

These should be considered when determining the IEP.

A discussion of every available test would be too lengthy for the purposes of this chapter. What should be noted is that there are numerous and varied standardized assessment instruments that should be used to thoroughly determine a child or adolescent's language ability. The examiner selected for this evaluation should be experienced and skilled in knowing which tests to select, how to administer and score them, how to interpret the data, and how to present the results as part of a cohesive evaluation. This thorough evaluation will benefit the individual being assessed, families, service providers, and will be functional and useful for qualifying for services through EI, CPSE, or CSE.

A critical part of the evaluation is the "summary and impressions" section. This summary is available to readers of the report across a variety of disciplines and experience; it must also be remembered that parents will be among the first to read the report. The final report should be written in a way that is understanable by all.

The diagnostic evaluation report will end with specific recommendations for speech and language therapy and related interventions to target associated areas of difficulty. The number of sessions per week, the length of each session, whether group or individual therapy is required, and the location of therapy (such as within the classroom or "push-in," outside the classroom, or at home) must be clearly specified. Strong justifications for the recommendations must be presented based on findings noted in the diagnostic report.

Recommendations might include therapies such as PROMPT (a motor program for children with apraxia) or therapies for oral-motor weakness, sensory issues, difficulties in auditory processing, etc. It should be noted that many children with Autism Spectrum Disorder begin speaking late due to of the difficulties and challenges presented in this chapter. Many of these children may display communicative intent; comprehend language; have receptive, pragmatic, and comprehension skills that exceed their expressive language skills; and be in need of a functional way to communicate.

Many children may begin with an assistive or augmentative communication system (AAC). These systems help children who may not be able to articulate the words they need but have the intent and skill to provide pragmatic functions, including requesting, negating, labeling or commenting. A system such as the Picture Exchange Communication System (PECS) allows a child to request using pictures that are exchanged for objects. This system is hierarchical, involves icons, and can be an effective means to reduce frustration and improve communication skills of children who are significantly behind in expressive language.

There are numerous other augmentative and assistive communication devices, including speech-generating devices (SGDs) that provide help in communicating, with many programs available on a computer, iPad, or similar devices. A program called Proloquo is frequently used and contains a system of icons that can be expanded to produce phrase- and sentence-length utterances. Dedicated assistive communication devices can be obtained based on the specific needs of the child. This is an area that should be addressed, if needed, by a skilled professional—usually a speech-language pathologist with expertise in this area. These systems should be incorporated into the IEP and school districts may pay for these devices.

Many parents are concerned that providing such a device will reduce or limit a child's ability to use oral language. Parents resist or deny use of such devices for children out of fear that they will continue to use them and not develop speech and language. It is important to stress that many evidence-based articles prove just the opposite. Research shows that providing such a system to a child reduces frustration, builds vocabulary, teaches the basis of interpersonal communication, and actually speeds the development of spoken language, if possible.

In summary, communication is a key area that must be properly assessed in working with individuals with Autism Spectrum Disorder. Indeed, language is the key to socialization, learning, and daily living. The acquisition of language also correlates directly with becoming more independent and self-sufficient.

Appendix E

Bullying Tips for Parents:
Q & A with Michael Dreiblatt of Nonprofit STAND UP to Bullying

Michael Dreiblatt (www.standuptobullying.org) is one of the nation's leading experts on bullying and speaks regularly on the topic. Below, Michael Dreiblatt answers some important questions that parents may have.

1. What is the role of bystanders in bullying? How can they help or hinder a bullying situation?

Most students are not bullies and most students do not get bullied on a regular basis. But bullying does happen and usually other students know about it. Most bullies prefer to have others around them to impress, receive encouragement from, or even join in the bullying. The people who see or are aware of bullying are referred to as "bystanders."

Bystanders might not appreciate the fact that they wield a great deal of power; enough power to help end bullying without putting themselves at significant risk. With a few simple strategies, bystanders can be a school's most powerful tool in stopping bullying in its tracks.

Ways That Bystanders Can Act to Stop Bullying:

Refuse to join in—visibly remove yourself

If the situation seems threatening or dangerous, it's best to stay clear of the bully. Even if it's not a dangerous situation, bear in mind that you don't have to listen to someone saying abusive things to another person. The best thing to do might be to calmly walk away. This will send the message that you do not support or respect this kind of treatment. It also may make the bully feel isolated.

Tell the bullies to stop—make bullying "uncool"

When bullying happens, other students usually see it or know about it. Therefore, students are in a great position to stop bullying—not only to help others, but to maintain safety for themselves. Bystanders can act in a way that communicates that the bullying is "not cool."

Find a way to separate the bully from the victim

Sometimes a bystander will have a friendship or other positive relationship with the bully. A bully need not be intrinsically evil. Many times, it will turn out that the bully has his or her own history of being bullied or abused. Sometimes a bystander can get the bully to stop abusive behavior just by changing the subject, distracting them, or finding something more fun or interesting to do.

Separate the victim from the bully

Sometimes a target of bullying is not sure what to do when being attacked; they may be nervous or flustered, just stand there and take it, or continue to read the cyber-attacks. In those instances, a bystander can remind the target to remove him/herself from the "line of fire." A bystander can help communicate to the victim that they are not required to "sign up" for victim status just because that is what the perpetrator wants—victims of bullying have more choices than they think they have.

Report to a trusted adult

Sometimes a bystander will know all about a bullying situation but hesitate to become involved. Every school should encourage its students to bring bullying situations to the attention of administration: "If you see something, say something." School systems should validate and reinforce bystanders who have the courage to take action or speak out.

2. What are the top danger signals that your child is being bullied?

If you are wondering whether your child is being bullied at school, trust your instincts. It is important not to jump to any conclusions, but if you are getting the feeling that bullying may be an issue, it is time to investigate. Investigating means first observing changes in behaviors or style. Observe your child's conversations, habits, rituals, and activities. Is your child complaining about feeling isolated or alone at school? Have you noticed a serious weight gain in a brief period of time? Have you noticed your child's pricey game collection slowly disappearing? Is your child avoiding an activity that once was happily anticipated? These are some warning signs that your child might be the victim of bullying. Be aware that not all children who are bullied exhibit warning signs.

Some warning signs your child may be the victim of bullying:

- Avoiding school, certain people, or places
- Increased complaints of being ill
- Being withdrawn/passive or being overly active and aggressive
- Missing or damaged property
- Frequent crying or feeling sad
- Signs of physical injury
- Suddenly receiving lower grades or showing signs of learning problems
- Major changes in behaviors including sleeping, eating, time alone, treatment of siblings, or complaining about school

3. Do some school systems succeed in the fight against bullying? What are they doing right?

Bullying can threaten students' physical and emotional safety at school and can negatively impact their ability to learn. The best way to address bullying is to stop it before it starts. Some school districts are controlling bullying by being proactive. There are a number of things that school staff can do to better prevent bullying:

Safe-School Planning Committees

Effective safe-school planning committees can decrease discipline problems, raise test scores, and help create a feeling of community. A well-rounded committee includes administrators, psychologists, school resource officers, teachers, and other personnel who have influence on safety and discipline on and off your school campus. The committee should also include representatives from the larger community, including parents and extracurricular activity leaders. Many high schools have found it useful to include health services organizations such as mental health agencies. Some high schools include student members, too.

When dealing with cyber-bullying, the safe-school committee should consider working with the informational technology or computer science department. Efforts should be coordinated between these departments and the safe-school committee in regard to technological requirements and other aspects of cyber-bullying or cyber threats.

Clearly Worded Policy
Most states offer model bullying prevention policies which include a definition of bullying, a range of consequences, and the requirements for school personnel who witness bullying behavior. Remember school district policy functions as school law, so make sure to seek good counsel when developing your policy.

Confidential Surveys
Surveys, particularly confidential surveys, are a useful way to collect data about the safety of your campus. This will yield valuable information concerning student behavior. By simply asking students about bullying or cyber-bullying, you raise awareness of the issue. Let students know that survey data will help shape the school or district's efforts to improve school safety. Surveys are also useful in determining areas of concern for school staff. Understanding how staff feel concerning their ability to respond effectively to security issues (including cyber-

bullying, harassment, and social aggression) will be especially useful in designing meaningful professional development.

Targeted Professional Development

Professional development should include teaching all staff a "same page" response if they encounter bullying on the school campus, in a school vehicle, or during extracurricular activities. For instance, a staff member needs to know how to effectively respond to a student who is bullying and how to respond to a student who reports bullying, as well as proper documentation procedures. Staff members will need to regularly practice these responses. A consistent and similar "same page" response will show the entire school community that such behavior is not acceptable nor tolerated by any adult anywhere on campus or during a school-sponsored function. In addition, it communicates respectful behavior and the values of the greater community.

Engaging Curriculum

Educators, parents, and mental health professionals have a responsibility to protect students from bullying of any form. Therefore, schools need to develop and implement meaningful curriculum to address bullying and the negative impact it has on students. Curriculum programs incorporating the direct teaching of values education; empathy training; the use of stories and drama; and "netiquette," (internet rules and expectations) all help to reduce bullying and cyber-bullying. Though this might seem like an added responsibility for the teacher or program coordinator, teaching respect, healthy choices, conflict resolution, and violence prevention are already part of the curriculum guidelines of all US states. Additionally, teaching these skills leads to classrooms with fewer interruptions and more time spent on-task, increasing actual learning time.

Often students are slow to hear these lessons because they interpret them as patronizing or condescending. Finding the right teacher for ongoing bullying prevention and cyber security lessons is equally important as finding an engaging curriculum. Occasional outside speakers and presentations allow the school's bullying lessons to be layered.

Supervision and Monitoring

Most schools have effective systems in place for monitoring bullying and cyber-bullying. When logging onto the school's network, have the screen display the code of conduct for internet usage. Have users agree to the code of conduct before they log on. Include notification that internet usage will be monitored. It is best to clearly communicate to students the time of day and areas of the school where cell phones and texting are allowed. These times and areas should then be monitored by staff to help ensure proper usage. Again, staff need to know how to respond if they discover a student using technology at the wrong time or place.

Sustained Parent and Community Outreach

When school personnel and parents communicate, they establish a stronger learning environment for the student at school and at home. Schools contact parents for many reasons including academic or behavioral difficulties, future plans for the child, or requesting parent volunteers. Now more than ever, schools and districts have ways to keep parents and community informed about behavioral expectations. School newsletters, parent information nights, and informative guest speakers are all effective ways to get community support behind your bullying prevention initiatives. School websites, blogs, E-newsletters, email, social media, and faxes all help to communicate information. Many local cable stations will put informational bulletins on their screens. Often, all you have to do is email the information to the station and they will take care of the rest.

Periodic Evaluation and Assessment

Since technology quickly changes and evolves, the methods used for bullying will also quickly change and evolve. Ongoing assessment of policies and procedures, student programs and curriculum, professional development, and community outreach will help ensure your cyber-bullying prevention program still is effective and up-to-date.

4. If your child is identified as being a bully, what do you recommend? What help is available for the bully?

If you hear from a teacher or another parent that your child is being a bully, the first thing you should do is talk to your child about the situation. Be direct about the issue but make it clear that you are open to hearing your child's side of the story. Say something along the lines of: "I got a call from the school today and the teacher indicated that you were involved in some bullying. I'm really concerned about this and we need to talk about it. Please tell me what happened."

If another parent approaches you about your child's bullying, notify teachers right away so they can be on the lookout for problematic behavior. Follow up with teachers regularly and give plenty of labeled praise when your child is being a good friend.

If your child has bullied other kids over the Internet, obtain passwords to their Snapchat, Instagram, Twitter, and other social media accounts and check them regularly to make sure that your child is behaving a respectful manner online. Be upfront about this: let your child know that you will be checking their social media activity until they prove that they can handle it responsibly.

Teach empathy, respect, and compassion. Children who bully often lack awareness of how others feel. Try to understand your child's feelings and help your child appreciate how others feel when they are bullied. Let your child know that everyone has feelings and that feelings matter. Encourage your child to take the perspective of the person who is being bullied. Ask your child: "Can you think of a time when you felt left out or sad because somebody wasn't being nice to you? That feeling you had is the same feeling your classmate is having because you aren't being nice to them." Help your child practice different ways of handling bullying situations. You can take turns playing the part of the child who does the bullying and the one who is bullied. Doing so may help your child understand what it's like to be in the other person's shoes.

Make your expectations clear. Let your child know that bullying is not okay under any circumstances and that you will not tolerate it. Let them know that there will be consequences for their behavior. Supply clear and consistent consequences for bullying. Be specific about what will happen if the bullying continues. Try to find meaningful consequences that fit the situation, such as loss of privileges or activities.

Confirm that your child's behavior is bullying and not the result of a disability. Sometimes, children with disabilities who have certain emotional and behavioral disorders or limited social skills act in ways that are mistaken for bullying. Whether the behavior is intentional or due to a disability, it still needs to be addressed. If your child with a disability is bullying, you may want to include bullying prevention goals in his or her Individualized Education Program (IEP).

If you are continually working on building friendship skills with your child and the bullying does not stop, seek a mental health evaluation. Your child might need a therapist's help to work through underlying issues.

5. What can teachers do to preempt or prevent bullying?

The first important thing to remember to do is what NOT to do: **Do not bully the bully.** This approach does not stop bullying. Bullying can garner strong emotional responses from everyone involved, including staff members who need to address the bully or bullies. It is especially important to be respectful and professional, role-modeling the behavior you expect from all your students. Discuss and teach specific behavioral expectations (both dos and don'ts). Teach and reinforce the skills needed, keeping in mind that some students may need extra one-on-one time to learn some of these skills.

Reward, on an individual basis and class basis, respectful behavior. Inform and explain to all students the consequences for breaking the rules. Keep in mind that consequences don't have to be punitive. Dole out consequences consistently, fairly, and respectfully. Consider developing specific plans for students who do not respond appropriately to standard consequences.

There is no one way to preempt all bullying, but a consistent response from staff members will create a school culture where all students understand that hurtful behavior will not be tolerated. By taking a proactive stance to reduce bullying behavior in schools, we can help prevent future incidents of school violence and keep our children safer.

NOTES:

NOTES: